Sexuality and People
with
Intellectual Disability

Sexuality and People with Intellectual Disability

SECOND EDITION

Lydia Fegan MA

*Clinical Psychologist/Team Leader, Client Services,
Autistic Association of NSW*

Anne Rauch BA

*Co-ordinator HIV/AIDS and Intellectual Disability
Project, Family Planning Association of NSW*

with contributions by Wendy McCarthy

·PAUL·H·
BROOKES
PUBLISHING Co

Baltimore · London · Toronto · Sydney

Paul H. Brookes Publishing Co.
PO Box 10624
Baltimore, Maryland 21285-0624

Library of Congress Cataloguing-in Publication Data
Fegan, Lydia.

*Sexuality and people with intellectual disability
by Lydia Fegan and Anne Rauch
p.   cm.
Includes bibliographical references and index.
ISBN 1-55766-140-5:
1. Mentally handicapped — Sexual behaviour.   2. Sex instruction for
the mentally handicapped.   I. Rauch, Anne.   II. Title.
HQ30.5.F44 1993
306.7'4 — dc20*   *93-20084*
                                                          CIP

Printed and bound in Australia

CONTENTS

PREFACE TO THE SECOND EDITION

The years since the first edition of this book have been an exciting, challenging and sometimes worrying time for people with intellectual disability, their parents and service providers. Deinstitutionalisation has continued and now most people with intellectual disability live in the community. Laws have been passed ensuring the rights of people with intellectual disability. With these changes have come an increased freedom for people with intellectual disability to exercise their sexuality. At the same time there has been the advent of AIDS, and a need for society to reevaluate its sexual practices and mores.

This second considerably expanded edition of *Sexuality and People with Intellectual Disability* has been written because there is now more than ever a need for people with intellectual disability, their parents and disability workers to be well informed about aspects of sexuality and people with intellectual disability. This edition, while maintaining a focus towards parents, has expanded this focus to include disability workers who are now more likely to be working in small community houses where they will have to deal with sexuality issues on a day-to-day basis.

The primary goal of the book is to assist parents and disability workers to support people with intellectual disability to understand and enjoy their sexuality. It does not attempt to answer every question, but it provides a comprehensive overview of issues that may arise. Suggestions are made as to where further information can be obtained. Additions to the previous edition include sections on training for menstrual management and masturbation, and chapters on Issues for Disability Workers, Being Sexually Healthy, Sexuality and Aging, Running a Formal Sex Education Program, Changing Inappropriate Sexual Behaviour and Sexuality and Autism.

The authors have been involved in educating and counselling people with intellectual disability, their parents and disability workers for the past two decades. The approaches in this book have been used successfully with people with mild, moderate and severe intellectual disability. We hope that you find it useful, and wish you every success in the rewarding and challenging process you engage in when you accept the sexuality of people with intellectual disability as an integral part of their self.

PREFACE TO THE FIRST EDITION

The material in this book is based on several years' experience working with health professionals, care-givers, institutional staff, parents and intellectually handicapped people themselves in consultative, counselling and educational roles.

It is intended as a guide for health professionals and parents to approaching questions about sex with those people who need extra special assistance in coping with their sexual growth and in learning to take care of themselves and each other.

All too often, the training of health professionals fails to provide them with practical guidelines for talking about sexual matters with their clients and, when faced with this task, they sometimes find themselves thrown back on to their personal attitudes and feelings, which are shaped by their family backgrounds. Some textbooks and some professionals have tried to deal with this question in very technical terms. We feel that a direct result of this approach is the frequent complaint we hear from parents who are disappointed and frustrated by the lack of a common meeting ground between themselves and the professionals who are meant to be helping.

In this book we have tried to steer clear of jargon and to get back to simple, practical language which solves the problem of communicating on such a difficult topic, rather than using language which contributes to further confusion, anxiety and disappointment.

We have particularly aimed the book at parents, many of whom feel they have missed out on practical help in coping with the sexual development of their intellectually handicapped children.

We would like to thank all those people who have helped us along the way, particularly Mrs. Winifred Kempton for her encouragement and support, Pamela Petty for her guidance and advice, Alan Gallaher for his time and his professional photographic skills, and Dennis and Norma, our touch-stones and advocates.

ACKNOWLEDGEMENTS

This book is enriched by the many people with intellectual disability, parents and workers who through our working and personal lives have shared with us their knowledge, feelings, desires, anxieties and aspirations.

The Family Planning Association of NSW has provided support for our work.

The interview with Julie and Robert was first published in an expanded form in On The Level Vol 1 No 2 pp 8–11.

Thanks also to Wendy McCarthy who collaborated on the First Edition, Pamela Petty our publisher for guidance, and special thanks to our families as it was our time with them that was taken to write the book.

Lydia Fegan

Anne Rauch

Chapter 1

SEXUAL RIGHTS FOR PEOPLE WITH INTELLECTUAL DISABILITY

A thirty-five-year-old woman living in a community residence run by a parent committee, had her male friend who worked with her stay the night. Residential staff respected her right to do so, but when the committee found out they reacted dramatically, prohibiting the visits and firing the man from the workshop.

A twenty-four-year-old man with no language, living in a group home, masturbated frequently. However he did not do it successfully to ejaculation and this appeared to increase his frustration and agitation. His parents firmly believed that masturbation was wrong and this made residential staff reluctant to raise the matter with them.

Our society has become increasingly concerned with the rights of people with intellectual disability. These rights have usually been viewed in terms of meeting basic human needs — good nutrition, appropriate living arrangements, recreational and educational opportunities, the right to work and the right to fulfill one's potential.

However, although it is generally agreed in principle that people with intellectual disability also have the right to sexual expression, there is still much uncertainty concerning the exact nature of such a right.

This is an especially difficult area for carers, in that the 'norms' of sexual expression in society are themselves not clear. In many cases they are entangled in misinformation and mythology, not to mention religious and cultural beliefs, and personal anxieties. This makes it difficult to know what is the range of options that can be considered

1

as reasonable or necessary to make available to people with intellectual disability. So while it is easy to sit down as a team — staff, parents and residents — and plan a daily schedule of mealtimes and reach consensus, it is not so easy to discuss whether it is alright for an adult in a group home to bring someone back for the night. Any such discussion will involve not only individual value systems, but also issues such as the extent of the duty of the carer and what constitutes sexual harassment and abuse.

Unfortunately, there are no ready solutions or answers in this area. All that we can do is gather as much information as possible so that we can be clear about the options available and the consequences of those options. This will enable us to ensure that those whom we care about and care for are also informed before they make their choices.

At the same time staff must be very clear as to their duty of care, and the laws of the particular state or country in which they work. But beyond that it becomes personal choice, and as long as there is no sexual exploitation, abuse or harassment, and no unreasonable encroachment on the lives of others, then staff and parents should be prepared to accept that sometimes people make choices which they do not agree with.

Many people with intellectual disability are disadvantaged with regard to sexual fulfilment and enjoyment. They need to be helped to better understand their sexuality and to incorporate this dimension of themselves into their lives as a whole. For such people the responsibility of parents and staff in their role as teachers of acceptable and appropriate social and sexual behaviour is vitally important.

This book was written in an effort to promote the right of people with intellectual disability to express their sexuality appropriately, and to assist those who share in their lives to facilitate this expression.

People with intellectual disability have varying degrees of reproductive ability, sexual interest, and sexual activity, as well as varying degrees of intellectual disability. They also show the same range of sexual response as the rest of the population. The fact that a person has a disability tells us little about the sexuality of that person. Yet the community at large, including carers and parents, often behaves towards people with intellectual disability as if they were also different sexually, with different sexual needs. In fact, the only real difference is their access to information — information about appropriate expression of sexuality, and appropriate communication of sexual needs.

One view that is still prevalent in some communities is that people with intellectual disability are delayed at the childhood level and therefore should be treated as children and protected from their own and others' sexual needs. Moreover, they should not be allowed to reproduce as they would be unable to rear their children and would thus place additional burdens on society.

According to this view the goal of sex education should be to control or eliminate sexual interest and expression. Sterilisation, restriction of privacy and efforts to ignore and even prevent masturbation all stem from this view.

In many cases this view arises out of genuine parental love and a desire to protect children from exploitation and abuse. Such parents truly believe that people with intellectual disability cannot be taught appropriate sexual behaviour.

It is true that levels of intellectual disability vary, meaning that needs in this area will likewise vary.

For some people it may be enough that they learn not to undress or touch their genitals in public, or to close the door when they are in the bathroom. Others may need to be informed about safe sex practices, or require relationship counselling.

The question is not whether a person with intellectual disability should be taught or informed about their sexuality, but how much information would actually be useful, and how best to teach it so that the information remains meaningful.

Sexual development is part and parcel of normal physical and emotional development, and should be acknowledged and respected as such, no matter what the level of intellectual disability.

Chapter 2
ISSUES FOR DISABILITY WORKERS

In the area of sexuality the role of the disability worker is, in some ways, quite different to the role parents play. This is because the attitudes that disability workers adopt in relation to their clients are governed by professional ethics, government policy, organisational policy, the policy of funding bodies and the management of the organisation.

This is not to say that staff do not have their own religious or moral viewpoints. Of course they do and they are entitled to them. However, at work they must enact the policies of the organisation for which they work.

For this reason, residential staff may need to spend some time sorting out their own attitudes to sexuality before they undertake teaching or reinforcing appropriate attitudes and behaviour with residents. They may have to come to terms with sexual behaviour which they personally find disturbing. For example, homosexuality may conflict with their religious beliefs, and yet the residential setting may include a homosexual couple. Or they may encounter instances of staff sexually abusing residents, and feel so confused that they turn a blind eye. Family Planning Associations and Planned Parenthood Federations can assist staff in developing stategies to deal with some of these difficult issues.

The main role of the disability worker in this area is to facilitate the social and sexual development of the person as part of his or her overall development. In some situations in Australia disability workers and disability services are responsible for ensuring that their clients have access to education about sexuality, and if a pregnancy or sexually transmitted disease occurred in a client through a worker's failure to ensure that appropriate education was provided, it is possible that the worker or service could be sued for negligence. This would not apply of course if the person with a disability had been given the information and then become pregnant or acquired a sexually transmitted disease.

In the United States disability workers and services are not generally liable if they fail to provide education about sexuality. However, case law does suggest situations where they might be held liable: for example, where an individual plan indicated that the service or worker would provide education and failed to do so, or where a service was aware of a risk and took no or clearly inadequate steps towards preventing it. For example, if a service was aware that a client was engaging in unprotected intercourse and if the client was unaware of the risk of pregnancy or sexually transmitted diseases, then the service would have a responsibility to make reasonable attempts to manage the risk, and sex education could be a part of these attempts.

The disability worker can facilitate the social and sexual development of a person with disability in a variety of ways. These include informal sex education, formal sex education and counselling. Informal sex education means using opportunities to teach as they arise and responding to questions. This is the kind of teaching that is usually required of disability workers. How to run a formal sex education program is covered in Chapter 21.

If a disability worker feels that he or she does not have the skills or the knowledge to deal with a particular issue, or feels unable to give the client an unbiased view of all the options, then the worker should refer the person to someone who is better able to deal with the issues. For example, if a worker is strongly opposed to abortion then he or she is unlikely to be able to give a pregnant woman with intellectual disability a balanced view of all her options. Another example might be where a worker feels that he or she lacks the expertise to deal with a victim of sexual assault.

Of course in some situations staff members will have to respond whether they want to or not, and in such cases their reactions should be consistent. An example would be if a woman brought a used menstrual pad into the lounge room or a man started masturbating in the lounge room.

Probably the most important aspect of a disability worker's job is interacting with clients on a day-to-day basis. Treating people as if they are deserving of respect, interesting and entitled to their own opinion can be of as much assistance in preventing inappropriate behaviour and promoting good social and relationship skills as any formal program. Other examples of appropriate informal teaching include respecting a person's privacy by, for example, knocking before entering, treating clients in an age-appropriate manner and modelling good behaviours.

It goes without saying that responsible sexual behaviour should be taught, reinforced and maintained in residential settings. In this respect there is clearly a necessity for consistency, so that residents are not confused. A set of simple guidelines covering the various aspects of sexuality and outlining what is required from staff, residents and parents can be very helpful in achieving such consistency.

A procedure for developing such a set of guidelines and some suggestions concerning content are given in Chapter 19. Suffice it to say here that these guidelines will work best if parents, staff and residents are all involved in their formulation, and if it is ensured that all new staff, new residents and new parents are informed of their contents.

In Australia, the United Kingdom and also in most states in America, some parents may have difficulty in coming to terms with the fact that if their child with intellectual disability is an adult, they have no legal right to impose restrictions on his or her sexual activity. In this area staff have a role in assisting parents to understand the sexuality of their son or daughter. This may involve reminding parents that their child is an adult with the same drives, needs and rights in regard to affection, relationships and sexual contact as other adults in the community. A person with intellectual disability also needs to learn socially appropriate behaviour and skills to avoid sexual assault and harassment. Of course, if the resident is still a child, his or her sex education can be decided by the parents alone.

Parents can assist staff by explaining their child's background in regard to sexuality. They can describe family attitudes to the developing sexuality of the person when he or she was growing up at home, and any relevant cultural or religious influences. Residents and parents can list the words used for body parts and functions, and outline attitudes to nudity, masturbation, having boyfriends and girlfriends, contraception, homosexuality and so on. This knowledge is important because it allows disability workers to assess and take into account individual levels of understanding concerning sex and sexual behaviour.

Occasionally a staff member may be required to accompany a person to a clinic for contraceptive advice, a pap test or a test for sexually transmitted diseases. In this situation the staff member can help in several ways: by providing emotional support, by advocating on the person's behalf, or by interpreting the information given by the doctor.

Chapter 3
ONE PARENT'S STORY:
A TAPED INTERVIEW

' "I answered the million dollar question last night. Thank God that's over!" '

'I have heard other parents say this quite often. But sex education isn't a matter of answering one question. Sex education should be part of growing up. More than anything, sex education is learning how to care for others. When I think of my own daughter, I hope that she will be able to cope with the responsibility of a relationship — the caring aspect of it. I hope that she will have an emotional relationship which brings the satisfaction and fulfilment that she needs, that we all need. I want to think that she was able to give to someone and that someone was giving back to her — and whether it was a man or a woman wouldn't matter.

'It is very difficult to teach that kind of caring. Children with intellectual disability are more protected at home — they don't often take an equal part in the family, they are not usually expected to help with the washing up or the setting of the table, nor are they often expected to take part in family conversations. And when they grow up, we expect them to be responsible straight away. Where on earth could they have learnt this responsibility? The other thing that makes it difficult is that people outside the family also tend to protect our children and to have low expectations of them. So your efforts to teach your children some responsibility at home are sometimes undermined at school.

'It's the same with sex, that's about responsibility too. It needs to be dealt with from an early age, just as it is with normal kids. Some parents don't agree; they sometimes say, "But my child doesn't understand very much, he gets confused, so there's not much point in talking about it." Another mother said that to me recently, and I asked her, "Does your son masturbate?" She said, "Yes," and I asked her, "Where does he do it?" and she said, "Oh, always in his own room with the door shut, we taught him that very early." As soon as she said that, I could see by the look on her face that she realised her son had understood that fundamental rule about privacy with masturbation and that it had begun to dawn on her that perhaps he could understand other things as well. Anyway, it doesn't matter if our children don't understand what we are saying. The point is that we, as parents, are getting into the habit of talking about sex openly, and it is the positive, caring attitudes we convey which count the most. Then, as the child matures, the understanding will deepen as well.

'The trouble is that we tend to give different messages about sex even when we are being open. It is very normal but you are not supposed to talk about it! It's a double message we all have to deal with, I guess. Like going to the toilet.

'When my daughter began menstruating, at first she wouldn't wear pads. She kept taking them out and throwing them away. I was at my wits' end. I thought I would have to buy lots of pants and sew pads into them. Eventually she accepted it, but then she wouldn't go to school when she had her period. She was very self-conscious about it and frightened that someone would notice. But you have to be patient and live through it all, knowing that it is only a stage and that it will pass as long as you are relaxed about it. Of course, it doesn't help when the teacher draws attention to it and says, in front of the whole class, "And Nancy, you must stop this nonsense of staying away from school when you are having periods!"

'There is a difference between being open about it and being so open that you lose the sense of privacy, or intrude on the privacy of others.

'Everyone should have information about sexual matters, particularly children with intellectual disability, but it's how it's given that's important. The emphasis must be on privacy and appropriateness and caring.

'There's not enough preparation of parents. Some parents need time to accept their child's development. They need help in reinforcing at home what their child might be learning at school. Health professionals are very important here. They must help the parents to view their child as a developing and growing individual who may well have the potential to lead an independent and fulfilling life as an adult, and to lay the groundwork for that possibility right from the start. Not reinforce the parents' fears of their child's limitations and incapacities.

'I know of a case where the parents of a girl with intellectual disability were told by the medical superintendent of an institution that they were placing her in, that they were not to worry about her sexual development as she would not have any, and that consequently there was no need for any sex education program. A few years later they were advised that they should consider a tubal ligation for their daughter as soon as possible, as the authorities suspected that she was, after all, capable of conceiving. That is a classic example of how not to go about the whole issue — health professionals giving parents the wrong information and then pressuring them into an irreversible decision in a crisis situation, with little or no attempt to include the daughter in that decision, or to give her any information about it. I know several parents who have had health professionals strongly advise them to consider vasectomies for their teenage sons, without giving them time to consider, or helping them to look at alternatives or to deal with their feelings.

'Staff who care for people with intellectual disability have a very great responsibility to make sure that they are not sexually exploited, either by other residents or by the staff themselves. Parents sometimes get very worried about this. Perhaps there are no grounds for their fears, but vague rumours float about and frighten them, and it is the responsibility of staff to help parents deal with these concerns and to reassure them. There might also be a need to improve the screening and training of staff who work in institutions.

'The other important question we have to look at squarely is who has the responsibility of teaching appropriate masturbation habits to people with severe intellectual disability. We have to tackle this question very soon because people in institutions are now going home more often, and it could cause a lot of problems. I know of a man who lives in an institution, who had a brief relationship with a girl in the same institution, and when she broke it off he became very frustrated. On his visits home his mother became very concerned about his tension and restlessness and irritability. She could tell he was sexually frustrated, and she knew he did not know how to deal with his frustration, but she could not teach him and there was no father in the picture who might be able to help.

'Another example I heard of was the case of a young boy who was masturbating a lot all the time in the most inappropriate places, by rubbing his thighs together when sitting down. So the staff at the institution attached sandpaper to the insides of his thighs.

'In some schools I know of, parents and teachers get together and develop a sex education program themselves for the children. Then it works beautifully, because the teachers feel that the parents are behind them, and the parents understand what is being taught at school and can follow it through at home.

'Parents have a right to demand appropriate services for their children, particularly in such a difficult area as sex. It is the area where their children are the most vulnerable because they are the least prepared to deal with it.

'People with intellectual disability must be taught to take care of themselves. There is no doubt that many do develop sexual needs sooner or later, just like everyone else. When they leave the protection of the home and begin to live an independent life, will they try to fulfil this need by exploiting others and allowing themselves to be exploited, or will they have already learnt that sexual expression is but one aspect of loving and caring and sharing?

'A lot of parents are afraid of sex education because they think that their children might be encouraged to try out behaviour they hear about in the sex education classes, such as masturbation or intercourse. But I know from my own experience that a good sex education program defines the acceptable limits. Another thing is that if the person is not at that point of development, then experimentation won't be important to them at all. And if people have sexual needs, then that is all the more reason to teach them how to cope with those needs appropriately.'

Chapter 4

THE PARENT AS SEX EDUCATOR

As far as the sex education of their children is concerned, parents have not had it easy, and this applies particularly to parents of children with intellectual disability. Our society's conditioning against speaking about sex has been so strong, for so long, that even today we still find some parents and other care-givers who are unable to broach the subject. Some parents still feel that their children should not be given information about sex because they will not be able to understand such information, or because it could be 'bad for them', 'give them wrong ideas' or 'overstimulate them', or 'because they are not old enough'.

Whether we like it or not we as parents are the sex educators of our children from the time they are born. We teach our children about sexuality and behaviour every day in an informal and incidental way. Children learn how to behave by observing their parents and by absorbing their parents' values. Despite all the information that can be obtained from a group sex education lesson, children will invariably only accept that information which is consistent with their parents' values and behaviour. Unless parents have been direct in their explanations, children may well misinterpret parental attitudes, especially when euphemisms and metaphors are used to deal with potentially embarrassing subjects. For children with intellectual disability, who may have difficulty understanding abstract concepts and symbolic representations, this can be even more confusing.

When to Start Sex Education?

There is no right or wrong time to start sex education. As we said earlier, education concerning sexuality starts from the moment a child is born. The main problem with teaching about sexuality is that it is usually too little and too late, because the children have already learned other things from their peers or from watching television.

Very young children are curious about their bodies and often examine their genitals and those of their siblings and friends. Parental reaction to this developing sexual curiosity is very important in conveying attitudes to sexuality. This curiosity is in no way unusual, nor is it a cause for alarm. Rather, such a situation should be seen as an opportunity to begin teaching appropriate behaviour, language and attitudes, such as not examining one's genitals in public.

It is also an opportunity to encourage the use of proper terms. For example, 'A boy's body is different from a girl's because he has a penis. A girl has an opening between her legs called a vagina. When she grows up she will have breasts like her mother. Both boys and girls when they grow up will have hair on their bodies.'

Inherent in this practical and objective approach is the notion of respect for the child's right to privacy. When children are taken to the toilet, the bathroom door should be closed. Parents should start teaching children to dress and undress in the bathroom or the bedroom from an early age. When children use deliberate exposure of their genitals as an attention-seeking device, it is usually because they have learnt that this behaviour can produce dramatic reactions from adults. A matter-of-fact approach to the child's body in the first place will guarantee that this sort of behaviour does not occur. Dramatic but positively reinforcing reactions should be directed only to the behaviours that adults want to promote.

From an early age, say three years old, parents should provide children with picture books about sexuality which are appropriate to their age. General access to such books is very helpful. It indicates to the child that the parents feel positive about sex, and that sexuality is a perfectly acceptable topic for discussion within the family. Dolls that are anatomically correct and instructive jigsaws are also good ways of integrating sex education into everyday life.

You can take advantage of opportunities that occur naturally to talk to your children about where babies come from, perhaps when you are pregnant or when a friend or neighbour announces her pregnancy. The earlier you start giving simple explanations, the easier it will be for the child to learn. Repetition is essential in teaching children about sexuality, just as it is in teaching them to say 'please' and 'thank you', or clean their teeth and brush their hair.

All children need to know how babies get started and what we mean by sexual intercourse or having sex, preferably before they are sexually mature. This is particularly important, not only to avoid misunderstandings, but also because children tend to absorb the ambiguous and worrying feelings and attitudes of the adults and children around them, and may themselves attribute negative connotations to the subject long before they reach puberty.

Parents should aim to be clear, simple and direct in their explanations. An appropriately simple explanation of the sexual act would be: 'A man puts his penis into a woman's vagina, which is the opening between her legs. Sperm comes out of his penis and goes into her vagina. If the sperm meets a tiny egg which is inside the woman's body, a baby will begin to grow. The baby grows in a place inside the woman's body called the uterus.'

Such an explanation is far less complex and much less confusing than statements like 'Daddy planted the seed', 'the stork brought you' or 'the doctors gave you to us'. It also means that the child understands the truth from the start and does not have to go back and unlearn myths about how babies are made and born.

When children understand the basic facts, you can use new situations to provide more information. For example, while listening to a song about love on the radio, you could make observations like: 'People don't have sex just to have babies. Usually they have sex because it feels good, because they enjoy it, and because it is a way of showing love and affection for each other. They like to hug and kiss.' This explanation can later be developed and made more explicit.

The child in puberty needs to know how hugging and kissing can lead to babies. For example, 'When a man feels excited his penis becomes hard and when a woman feels excited her vagina becomes moist. Sometimes when a man and woman are excited they may decide to have sexual intercourse. Then the man puts his penis into the woman's vagina and moves it back and forth, usually until semen squirts from his penis into the vagina. This is called ejaculating. Sometimes it is called having an orgasm. It is usually a very exciting time. In the sticky stuff, called the semen, which comes out of the man's penis, there is sperm and it is the sperm which is needed to make babies.'

The explanation of a woman's sexual excitement could follow these lines: 'A woman also becomes sexually excited when she has intercourse. Above her vagina she has a special sensitive spot called the clitoris. When it is touched or rubbed gently in a certain way, it makes her feel very good. When a woman becomes sexually excited, her vagina becomes moist. This helps the man's penis to slip inside it. When a woman has an orgasm the muscles in her vagina squeeze together and she experiences feelings of intense excitement and pleasure. People usually feel very relaxed and contented after they have had sex together. Having sex is also often called "making love".'

In talking about sexual intercourse you not only provide information but also impart values. You might say something like: 'Not everyone has sexual intercourse — some people don't feel the need to have it. Others never meet anyone they like enough. Having sex with someone is very special. People should only have sex when they really care about each other and when both really want to do it. Sex should never be used to hurt somebody.

'Many people believe you shouldn't have sex unless you are married and some people go through their whole lives without having sex, or getting married. Just because you are close to someone doesn't mean you have to marry them or have sex with them.

'If you choose to have sex with someone, that person should also want to have sex with you, and you should do it privately. Having sex is not a public event. It is something that is shared between two people in private. To force someone to have sex is unloving, distressing and painful. It is also illegal which means that you can go to jail for it.'

All parents have a responsibility to explain their moral standards to their children. If you firmly believe that people should not have sex before they are married, you should say so. If your children know what your standards are, then they have a framework to work within. It also helps them to understand why other people have standards. If your standards are based on strong religious or cultural values, then you should explain these values to your children. They are far more likely to accept your standards if they understand the basis for them. In this process, differences can emerge even between partners, and it is necessary to resolve these. Like other people, people with intellectual disability need special guidance in developing their values.

The rules applied to the sexual behaviour of people with intellectual disability are often far stricter than the rules applied to the rest of the community. There may be very good reasons for this. As a parent, you may be afraid that your child could be exploited or abused. However, it's worth making sure now and then that you understand why you have a double standard. If it's a double standard which limits the growth and development of your child, it might be time to relax the standard a little. Is your child with intellectual disability allowed to go out with people of the opposite sex? Is he or she growing up with an appropriate amount of responsibility? It may be possible to organise outings with the opposite sex under supervision.

When your children reach adulthood you may feel nervous about your ability to control or protect them. Fear of pregnancy is a valid concern. So is sexual assault. It is a matter of taking careful note of the risks involved and confronting the issues in a responsible manner.

Children with intellectual disability tend to remain at home much longer than most children. However, this does not mean that they should not be allowed to take risks and make mistakes too. This requires a very delicate balance between supervision and leaving room for risk-taking. If you never allow your child to take risks, you may protect him or her from some pain, but you will also exclude him or her from the pleasures of exploring relationships and learning to become an adult.

It is essential to start thinking about a more formal sex education program before the person with intellectual disability reaches puberty. And if a person is to move out of home into a community-based home, then a sex education program should be an integral part of his or her preparation for community life.

Formal Sex Education

The best teachers are those who feel confident and at ease, and can be open and direct about the subject. Here is a check list to help parents become more effective sex educators.

- Become aware of your own attitudes — are they the result of the way you learned about sex? Would you have preferred to learn about sex in a different way? Do your ideas about sex and sexual behaviour now differ from those of your parents? Do you have strong religious views which influence your attitude towards sex? Have your sexual experiences been positive and pleasant? Do you expect your children to adhere to your sexual standards? Do you have friends whose lifestyles, sexual preferences and attitudes towards sex differ from your own? Do you worry that these people might influence your children?

- How up-to-date is your factual information about sex? When was the last time you read an article or a book about sex? Do you keep in touch with what young people are learning about sex these days?

- You should try to share your fears and concerns with other parents — fears about how you will cope if your child behaves inappropriately, about your child's safety, sexual exploitation, pregnancy, sexually transmitted diseases and so on. Getting together with other parents who are in the same predicament will help you understand how other parents cope. It will also make it easier for you to overcome any discomfort you feel when talking about sex.

- Invite a sex educator to help your parent group get started. An experienced sex educator will soon make it easy for you to talk about sex and will be able to help you find answers to many of your concerns.

- As you become more comfortable with the topic, you can begin to rehearse questions and answers about sex with your partner or with other parents. Try to explain menstruation or wet dreams in the simplest possible terms. Use some of your children's slang expressions — don't be upset if your children use slang words for penis and vagina — everyone else does. Note that this does not mean that children should not be taught the correct terms at an early age, but they do need to know the slang terms used by their peers.

- Do not assume that once formal education has taken place there is no need for informal repetition and reinforcement. Be prepared to repeat and reinforce your positive statements about attitudes and appropriate behaviours at every opportunity.

- Provide visual instruction whenever possible. Videos and slides are available from Family Planning Associations and Planned Parenthood Federations, Health Departments and schools. Video viewing is an excellent group activity, even with just three or four children. Many centres also provide charts, slides, books, menstrual kits, jigsaws, anatomically correct dolls and audio-tapes.

- Don't be too serious. It is not necessary to know everything — providing even some information will set your child on the right path. If you can deal with sexuality on a day-to-day basis, just as you do with nutrition, safety and courteous behaviour, it becomes a less threatening subject for both you and your child. Try to keep your sense of humour — laughter helps everyone relax.

- Let your child know that there are many possible lifestyles. Don't narrow the options.

As in all things, parents have the right to expect that other carers, including teachers, will have the same approach to the sex education of their child as they have. To ensure that there is consistency across all the child's environments parents must tell other carers what their attitudes and strategies are in the home. How this can be done is discussed in more detail in Chapters 18 and 19.

Chapter 5
HELPING WITH GROWING UP

Helping with growing up means helping your child to become an independent man or woman, one who can take care of him or herself and take responsibility for his or her own life. Eventually it may also mean taking responsibility for others, living away from the protection of parents and making independent choices.

No matter how limited a person with intellectual disability may be in the skills that he or she can acquire, every person is capable of taking responsibility for certain aspects of his or her life. But unless children are given opportunities to learn how to handle a variety of responsibilities and choices during their growing up years, no one will ever know how much potential they have to achieve independence.

Overprotected children often learn only a limited set of behaviours and thus never acquire the dignity that comes with being able to cope with a variety of experiences. It is worth remembering that about 90 per cent of people with intellectual disability are only mildly disabled and have the potential to lead largely independent lives.

Teaching young children to dress and wash themselves, whether they are intellectually disabled or not, can take a long time and it is tempting for parents to do it for them. For the parents of a child with intellectual disability it can seem an unending process. Patience and tempers snap as they wait for children to brush their hair, or put on a shoe. To get through some of the early frustrations of teaching self care it can be helpful to use a team approach which includes other members of the family, outside carers and disability workers and teachers.

Teaching children to look after themselves pays off in the end. Whenever possible, try to give yourself enough time for teaching activities so that you will not be rushed and irritable. Establishing some sort of schedule or routine for your child will be a great help. Dressing up, a game much loved by children, is a wonderful way of teaching your child how to dress and how to select clothes. Some-

times people think that concern about clothes is frivolous and irrele-
vant, but the way your child presents to the outside world is critical
to being accepted in the community. The child with intellectual
disability deserves as much care as possible to help attract positive
rather than negative attention.

Visits to the hairdresser are important in encouraging children to
look after their appearance. Exercise and diet are also important and
can help remove many differences between the non-disabled and
disabled, as well as increase self-esteem.

It is important to instill healthy eating habits at an early age. As the
provider of food and drink, it is your responsibility to make sure that
soft drinks and fast foods are only available on a limited basis.
Establish a routine of only providing such food on a particular day in
the week or month and teach your child to wait for that time. You
can even use these occasions as a reward for achieving some behaviour you are trying to teach. Do not keep foods like chocolate, sweet
biscuits, chips and so on on view in the cupboard. Very early in
your child's life it may be a good strategy to work out a set of
guidelines about how and what you will feed your child — then
keep to it.

It is also a good idea to schedule a variety of exercise activities
into your child's life. Walking, swimming, dancing and gentle aero-
bics are all good activities. Such exercise will not only increase your
child's fitness and number of leisure activities, but also provide an
avenue for integration into mainstream group activities.

As children approach puberty, the necessity for cleanliness needs
to be stressed over and over again. You can explain in simple terms,
like this: 'Teenage boys and girls sweat more as their bodies change
and the sweat can cause unpleasant smells. It is important that you
shower each day and wear clean clothes.'

Both boys and girls should be taught to use a mild underarm
deodorant. Teenage acne can become a problem, so washing the
face regularly with soap and water should be encouraged. Learning
to shave can be a way of giving boys an added feeling of control
over the way they look. Electric razors are probably easier to use
than safety razors. If a boy has poor co-ordination, it may be possible to fit the electric shaver with a handle to make it easier to hold.
If moustaches are in fashion, your son may enjoy growing one, or
perhaps he would prefer a beard. Certainly these measures will add
to his sense of individual identity and self-esteem.

Remember too that, like adults, children enjoy having a place that
is their own — a place, such as a bedroom, which other members of

the family respect as being the child's private area. If you knock on the door of the bathroom or bedroom when your child is inside, the child will be encouraged to show the same courtesy to you and to others.

Helping with tasks around the house is an important source of self-esteem. Most children can learn to make their beds, pick up their toys, set the table, make sandwiches, fold clothes, wash dishes and run the vacuum cleaner. The positive feedback that they receive from being helpful gives them a feeling of importance and responsibility.

A good strategy to teach your child tasks around the house is to break the task down into small steps and teach one step at a time. This method gives both you and your child a lot of little rewards along the way. If some of the steps are too difficult for your child to learn, then you may need to break the step down into even smaller bits. You may also need to teach your child to ask for help when he or she needs it. You might find it useful to attend a short course on behaviour management techniques. Your child's teacher or social worker should be able to put you in touch with appropriate parent training courses.

Another important skill that people with intellectual disability have to learn is self-protection. This includes being able to distinguish between appropriate and inappropriate touching and between those who are allowed to touch and those who are not, and also when it is important to tell someone that a person is touching them inappropriately and who to tell. One technique that is used to teach people to distinguish between appropriate and inappropriate touching is to designate all areas of the body that are covered by underwear or a swimsuit as private or not-to-be-touched areas.

'Stranger danger' is a difficult concept to teach. Role-plays with people dressing up as strangers and varying the approach is one way. Organising a 'stranger approach' situation in the street, using a family friend who is not known to your son or daughter while you watch from a distance, can be used to evaluate whether the concept has been understood.

Unfortunately research shows that most instances of sexual assault are perpetrated by people who are known to the child. This makes it all the more important to ensure that your child is able to distinguish between appropriate and inappropriate touching, and is able to communicate any fears or need for help to others. The teaching program 'Circles Concepts' can be very helpful in imparting these important skills.

The Circles Concept

Relationships are an integral and vital part of an individual's life.

The Circles Concept is an approach developed specifically to teach people with intellectual disability about the degrees of intimacy in different relationships. It can be used to teach about appropriate touching and together with training in assertiveness skills can assist people with intellectual disability to identify when they are being sexually exploited and to act to protect themselves.

It was originally developed in the United States and is now widely used in Australia. The Resources section in this book will identify where you can get additional information about it.

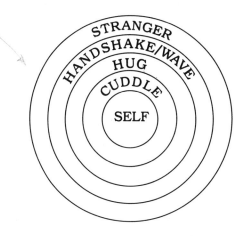

Some of the ideas or themes that can be built into the Circles Concept are as follows:

- You are unique — everyone has their own individual set of circles.
- People don't always have someone in every circle all the time.
- Different behaviour is appropriate in different circles.
- People can shift circles in either direction.
- Usually it is best if people don't move from an outer circle (e.g. stranger) to an inner circle (e.g. cuddle) immediately.
- No one can come into your inner circles unless you want them to be there.
- You cannot enter another person's inner circles unless they want you to be there.

- You have the right to say no if someone is trying to enter your inner circles and you don't want them there.
- Usually, only one very special friend such as a boyfriend/girl-friend/husband/wife is able to enter your own self circle in order to have sex.
- Relatives do not come into the self circle; that is, it is not okay to have sex with your relatives.

The categories of people who can come into the various circles are:

- Cuddle circle — boyfriend, girlfriend, husband, wife and immediate family if they are close.
- Hug circle — very good friends.
- Handshake/wave circle — neighbours, workmates, acquaintances.

However, this is very individual and the circle people can come into depends more on how close the relationship is than the type of person they are.

Workers or parents can present the Circles Concept on a one-to-one basis or in group education. It is often taught in special schools. Slides or pictures can be used. You will need a piece of material or large piece of cardboard with circles drawn on it to place on the floor or a table. Explain or demonstrate using photos and pictures, or a story, which categories of people are in each circle and what the appropriate behaviours are to show towards these people.

For example, you could have a picture or a photograph of a woman you call Jenny. Her boyfriend John could go in her cuddle circle. So could her father if the relationship is close. However, although John can enter Jenny's self circle if they both decide they want to have sex, Jenny's father can't. Jenny's good friends go in her hug circle, and so on. With each new person, you can introduce a new photograph or picture. You can also use pictures showing appropriate behaviour between Jenny and these people.

As stated previously Circles can also be used to teach protective behaviours. It is not okay for other people to show or do a behaviour that the other person does not want, and vice versa. For example, sometimes people try to touch people with intellectual disability or have sex with them when they don't want to, even people they like. The person with intellectual disability can say no.

Circles can also be used to teach about public and private body parts, places and behaviours. Private parts of the body are usually those covered by underwear. They can only be shown in the self circle (with the exception of doctors and personal care attendants when these are required). A private place is where a person is on his or her own or with a boyfriend/girlfriend/husband/wife and no one else will come in. A public place is where other people can be or go. Private places are in the inner circle and public places further out.

Parents and workers can use picture cards with places, behaviours and people on them and ask people with intellectual disability to place them in the appropriate circles. Role-plays and real life situations can be used to reinforce learning.

The number of circles would usually be reduced when teaching a person with severe intellectual disability.

Growing Up Female

For a girl with intellectual disability, growing up can be a very anxious time, especially when she begins to undergo the physiological changes of puberty. To see hair suddenly growing under the arms and on the genital area, the breasts growing bigger, and the blood of the first period, can be very frightening and confusing, especially if there has been no preparation. It is very important to prepare a girl gently and patiently for these changes so that she can adjust without unnecessary stress.

It is a good idea to begin such preparation for puberty early — at least by the age of nine. Here is one way you could approach the subject:

- 'See how the hair is beginning to grow under your arms and between your legs on your genital area, and how your breasts are growing — that means you are growing up to be a woman, just like your mum (your big sister, your auntie).'
- 'Soon you will also see some blood coming out of your vagina — that also means that you are growing up. All grown-up women have that blood coming out of their vagina for a few days every month. It is called having a period. It means that your body will be able to make a baby when you are ready to start a family of your own.'
- 'As soon as you see the blood coming out you must come and tell me or your teacher, so that we can take you to the bathroom and help you to clean it up and put a pad on.'

- 'Let's go into the bathroom now and I will show you how to clean yourself and put a pad on, as if you were having a period.'
- 'You don't tell everyone that you are having a period. It is something that is very special and private.'
- 'Sometimes you will feel a sort of ticklish feeling around your vagina that will make you want to touch and rub it. You should wait until you can go into your bedroom to do that, because it is a very special and private feeling. You should not touch yourself on the vagina in public. This is called masturbation and it can only be done in private.'
- 'Another thing that happens as you grow up is that your breasts start getting bigger. Soon you and I will have to go shopping for bras. Bras are a form of underwear, like panties, which women wear around their breasts under their clothes.'

Growing Up Male

Boys are also affected by the hormonal changes associated with puberty. At this time some boys will feel an increase in energy while others will experience heightened irritability, agitation and even aggression. This may be an expression of an increase in physiological frustration which could be eased through masturbation. However, sometimes an increase in aggression is the result of a growing physical strength which the boy cannot handle. In this case frightened or punitive reactions can create a vicious circle, reinforcing the inappropriate behaviour and even escalating it.

Physical changes and growth of body hair can best be explained by giving the boy an opportunity to see his father (or older brother) naked. This will give the boy some indication of the future shape and texture of his own body. It is important to actually tell him that his body is going to change in that way rather than leave it to him to figure it out for himself. This could be difficult for him to understand so you may have to keep repeating it. As the changes occur, you can confirm them, and respond to them positively. Here is one way you could describe the changes:

- 'Hair will grow under your arms and around your penis and then on your face. It will feel different from the hair on your head.'
- 'Your penis and testicles will grow larger and from time to time your penis will get hard and stick up. Sometimes this will seem to happen for no reason at all; other times it will happen when you are thinking about sex or girls or when you read something

in a magazine. It can be embarrassing but it happens to all men. It is called an erection. An erection is a private thing. Do not ask everyone to look at it. Eventually it will go away.'

- 'Sometimes you will wake up in the morning and think you have wet the bed because all the sheets are wet and sticky. You haven't wet the bed — some semen has come out of your penis during the night. This is called a wet dream. Wipe the semen off with a tissue and wash yourself. Put your pajamas and sheets out to wash or air if they are messy.'

- 'The semen that comes out of your penis has sperm in it which can help make a baby. Your body makes sperm all the time.'

- 'It is okay to think about sex or to dream about it. Everyone does. Dreams, thoughts and fantasies cannot hurt you or anyone else.'

- 'Lots of boys feel the need to rub their penis when they get an erection. That's fine. All men feel like that. It is called masturbation and can only be done in private. You should not touch your penis in public. You should wait until you can go somewhere private.'

There is more detailed information about masturbation and menstruation in the following chapters.

Chapter 6
MASTURBATION

'Sexual self pleasuring or masturbation is a natural part of sexual behaviour for individuals of all ages. It can help to develop a sense of the body as belonging to the self and an affirmative attitude towards the body as a legitimate source of enjoyment. It can also help in the release of tension in a way harmless to the self and to others.'

Sex Information and Education Council of the United States (SIECUS).

Masturbation can become a serious issue if parents, teachers, caregivers and disability workers differ in their ideas about what constitutes permissible behaviour. For example, how can a teacher train a child to masturbate in private if the parents permit the child to masturbate anywhere at home? How can workers relieve children's guilt about their sexual feelings if parents punish them for masturbating? Such conflict troubles both professionals and parents and is very difficult to resolve.

It is worth remembering that the goal is to help people with intellectual disability achieve a positive attitude towards their sexuality and, at the same time, to teach them acceptable social behaviour. It is necessary to make them aware that masturbation is not a public activity, but this needs to be done without giving negative connotations to the act itself, or making the person feel bad.

Masturbation is a natural part of sexual development. Young children want to find out what their bodies feel like. They like to put fingers in their noses and in their eyes, and their genitals get the same sort of treatment. Such exploration is part of the discovery of the body. If it provides a person with pleasure, it is not unnatural for them to want to repeat it. The following is a summary of our views on masturbation:

- Masturbation is normal and is to be expected.
- Masturbation is harmless and, very possibly, beneficial.
- Punishing someone physically or verbally for masturbating can be damaging to that person.
- People with intellectual disability, like everyone else, are likely to turn to whatever sources of distraction, amusement or escape are available to them when bored.
- Masturbation does not cause brain damage, retardation, physical handicaps, impotence, insanity or any other aberrations attributed to it.
- Intellectual disability does not cause people to masturbate.
- All kinds of people masturbate, regardless of race, religion, sex, age and mental ability.

It may take a great deal of patience and perseverance on the part of parents to take their children, even as adults, to their room every time they start to masturbate. It is important to stress to the child that he or she is not being reprimanded for masturbating, only for doing it in the wrong place. If they can learn to distinguish between things people do in public and things people do in private, such as going to the toilet, bathing and undressing, then they can learn that masturbation is done in private. If a person is masturbating frequently, that is, to the point where parents are concerned, the situation may need to be investigated. It may be that the person does not know how to gain relief from masturbation, or that the person is bored and has few other stimulating activities. There is also the possibility of a vaginal infection or a rash on the penis causing discomfort.

Let us now consider how we might explain masturbation to children. Do not assume that all children know how to masturbate simply because you observe them rubbing or exploring their genitals. You may still need to explain how they can achieve sexual release.

You could begin as follows: 'Almost all boys and girls (men and women) masturbate. It's fine to masturbate if you do it in a private place.'

To your son, you could say: 'Men masturbate by putting their hand around their penis and pulling it up and down quickly until they get a nice, warm, relaxed feeling. Eventually, white, sticky fluid called semen comes out of the penis and this is called ejaculation. Then the penis gets soft again and the man feels relaxed. It is a good idea to have a handkerchief or a tissue handy to wipe up the semen. There are many slang words for masturbation, such as "jerking off".'

To your daughter you might say: 'Women usually rub a very sensitive spot just above the vagina which is called the clitoris. It feels good to touch the spot gently with the fingers. Some women like to put a finger in their vagina and move it back and forth, or cross their legs and rub their thighs together. When a woman gets excited, her vagina gets wet inside but the wetness doesn't spurt out. A woman's orgasm happens when she becomes very excited and the muscles in her vagina squeeze together quickly a number of times. Some women and men have daydreams or fantasies about sex when they are masturbating.'

Some people with intellectual disability and some people with autism are unable to masturbate to climax. This may make them very frustrated, uncomfortable and irritable and can lead to aggressive behaviour and sometimes to a return of toileting problems. In this situation it can be helpful to teach the person how to masturbate to climax. However, it is necessary to be careful as the distinction between sex education and sexual abuse may become blurred. Before embarking on any masturbation education program it is important to acquaint yourself with the laws in your country or state regarding abuse, assault and informed consent.

In general, the strategies used to teach other skills can also be adapted to teach masturbation. You could use a sequence of pictures, verbal commands, photographs, slides, a video or an anatomically correct doll. Some people learn best by modelling what another person is doing. However, this is illegal in some states and countries. Similarly, the technique of using a mirror to demonstrate to a woman how to touch her clitoris with her fingers may be illegal. In both cases, the informed consent of the person with intellectual disability may be necessary.

A hand-held vibrator can be helpful in teaching masturbation. The session might start with the person being shown how to use the vibrator as a massager all over the body. Again, visual cues such as pictures can be useful. A vibrating pillow is another useful device. It can be held on top of the genital area with the person lying on his or her back or the person can lie on top of it on the stomach.

Some people with intellectual disability may need to be helped to slot time for masturbation into their daily routine. For example, the person could go to bed a little earlier than usual on some nights, or be scheduled a 'private time' on the weekends. This scheduling is an entirely individual thing. If the person is unable to communicate and is demonstrating inappropriate choices regarding times and places for masturbating, then careful observation will soon reveal when is the most appropriate time for that individual to have a 'private time'.

It is worth noting that some men find a wet bed distressing, as they confuse semen with urine. This can be difficult to explain and it might be easier for the man to masturbate while sitting in an arm-chair in his room, or while in the shower.

Some people recommend that men learn to masturbate with a condom on. There are several good reasons for this. It keeps the bed dry, it is easier to clean up afterwards and, if the person later shows a desire for sexual intercourse, the use of a condom in connection with sexual arousal will already have been taught.

The following is a possible sequence of verbal steps which might be used as a guide when teaching someone how to masturbate. Naturally, it is only to be used in the privacy of the person's bedroom. The steps could be associated with photographs, line drawings, pictures or a video.

- Take pants off.
- Put cushion on bed. (Indicate where).
- Lie on stomach on top of cushion.
- Rock from side to side.

This is only a brief example, and does not include a number of other steps which would need to be included in order for the program to be complete. You might prefer to prepare the person on the bed, then switch on the vibrating cushion, the vibrator, or video, and leave the room for twenty to thirty minutes.

It is true that some people, including people with intellectual disability, do not have very strong sexual urges. But if there are clear signs that the growing adolescent or young adult is becoming sexually restless, then it is important to do something about it.

One father expressed great concern at a seminar about his son's habit of waking up in the middle of the night once or twice a week and trying to climb into the parents' bed. His father had noticed that on every occasion his son had an erection. He would lead him back to his own bed, but the next morning there was no sign that ejaculation had occurred. This had been going on for some months at great inconvenience to the parents. The parents also felt that their son was becoming more irritable.

In this case it was fair to assume that the boy was experiencing sexual tension which he was unable to relieve, and that he was turning to his parents for help. Once the father taught his son to masturbate, the nocturnal visits stopped.

Some people with intellectual disability do not reach sexual ma-turity till their early twenties. By that time they may be living in a group home and the staff may then be confronted with the issue of teaching masturbation skills. That is why parents have such an important role to play in preparing their son or daughter for community living.

Demonstration on oneself whether as a staff member or a parent or other relative, or on the body of the person with intellectual disability, is likely to be illegal unless the person has consented. Usually the use of videos, slides, pictures and anatomically correct dolls will be sufficient to demonstrate technique. It is much more appropriate, however, to include the teaching of masturbation in a program designed by a suitably qualified professional. If there are continuing difficulties, it may be appropriate to contact a sex therapist through one of the agencies mentioned below.

We have mentioned a number of aids which can be useful. The agencies which can help you with courses, resources, advice and counselling are Family Planning Associations, Planned Parenthood Federations, and Societies for Sex Educators, Researchers and Therapists (AASERT in the United States, and ASSERT in Australia). Some service organisations for people with intellectual disabilities or autism can also be helpful with advice or even programs and aids. In the United States the Autism Society of America and the Association for People with Intellectual Handicaps may be able to advise you on the appropriate organisation in your state.

We do understand that many parents would find it impossible to follow through on any of the above strategies. The agencies mentioned above may be able to recommend professional counsellors who could help.

Chapter 7
MENSTRUATION

'My periods started when I was eleven years old. Mum never told me that girls get periods. I started getting sick when I was at school and when I got home I had blood on my pants. Then Mum just told me that all girls get that.'

Narelle

This book is based on the view that sex education is education about human sexuality. It is a process of learning about being male and female, about the totality of being human. Sex is not just sexual intercourse; it's not what an individual does, but what he or she *is*. Every individual's self image is inseparably tied to his or her sex and to his or her development as a male or a female. For girls with intellectual disability, growing up can be a very anxious time indeed, especially when they begin to undergo the physiological changes of puberty. To see the blood from their first period without preparation can be very frightening and confusing for them. Like other girls in our society, girls with intellectual disability have to be lovingly and patiently prepared for menstruation so that they can be trained and educated to manage it. Withholding information only causes fear and anxiety.

It is a good idea to begin preparation for menstruation early — at least by the age of nine. You might tell your daughter that menstruation will begin after breast development and the growth of pubic hair. You can say that these are the signs to look for and reassure her that you will be around to help and make her feel positive about her first period. It is very important that your daughter knows she should tell someone at home or her teacher at school when she sees blood on her pants for the first time. She will need to learn, probably through repeated tellings and demonstrations, how to manage sanitary napkins and that this should be done privately. Explain to her that menstruation is a sign of her becoming a woman and a positive sign that she is successfully growing up. This is also a good time to begin discussions on the connection between fertility and menstruation.

Some children find the word 'menstruation' difficult to cope with and difficult to pronounce, and the term 'period' may be easier. Wherever possible, girls should be able to recognise both words. It gives them an added feeling of security when other people use the terms with them. Family Planning Associations, Planned Parenthood Federations, Community Health Centres, Departments of Education and Family Life Movement Centres will be able to help with pictures, slides, menstrual kits and other educational aids, and some manufacturers of sanitary napkins and hygiene products may also have educational aids. If it can be arranged for your daughter's school to use some of these, this would be an excellent way to start a small group discussion about menstrual management. It's also a way of demonstrating that everyone is in the same boat.

Many parents ask us whether boys should also be told about menstruation. We recommend very strongly that boys be made aware of the changes that girls undergo in puberty, particularly boys in families where there is a person with a learning difficulty who is menstruating. Brothers can often be observant and helpful, for example if a girl is unaware that she has a blood stain on her dress. A boy who knows why this has happened can be very solicitous of and helpful to his sister. Moreover, boys are bound to see the evidence of menstruation in the household and it is a good idea to include the whole family in what is an integral part of growing up and understanding fertility. It is also important that boys learn to respect girls' need for privacy.

Many parents doubt that their daughter with intellectual disability will be able to change a sanitary pad on her own. We believe that a girl who is capable of going to the toilet by herself can learn to do this. If she has watched her mother or older sister remove a used pad, wrap it in toilet paper, put it in the wastepaper basket and replace it with a new pad, she can imitate the sequence. She is also learning that this is a normal function.

One way of teaching women with intellectual disability to manage their periods and change their own pads is to break the process down into a series of discrete tasks and teach these one at a time. Even women with severe intellectual disability can learn to manage their own menstruation if taught in this systematic way.

This teaching can begin before a woman begins menstruating.

Some women with intellectual disability are able to generalise to their own period after watching another woman change her sanitary pads. Other women benefit more from watching and then imitating the sequence themselves. This teaching should always be done in a bathroom or toilet.

In some cases it may be easier if the pre-menstrual program is carried out by a female teacher at school. Naturally, a pre-condition for this is an understanding and sensitive teacher. The teacher is likely to have the training to set up and implement programs, and she can sort out any problems which arise before the program is transferred to the home.

The following are some points to consider before embarking on a pre-menstrual program:

- A female teacher.
- Good communication and teamwork between parent and teacher.
- Parent-teacher meetings so that both parties fully understand what routines can be realistically established at home, and which procedures the mother wants the child to learn.
- The circumstances have to be prepared such that the program can be carried out regularly under supervision for its duration.
- The thickness and size of the pads should be increased gradually so as to give the girl time to get used to wearing them.
- The girl's progress through the learning steps should be charted. This makes it easier to see where any difficulties are being experienced.

The cue for any woman to use a menstrual pad or sanitary napkin is the appearance of blood on her panties. This cue can be simulated using red food colouring and the woman can be taken through the following steps:

- When the young woman sees blood on her panties she should get a pad and panties from a designated place. At home this will usually be from a drawer or cupboard in the bathroom; at work she should always keep a pad and panties in a paperbag in her handbag.
- Go to the toilet.
- Take off the soiled panties and put them in the washing basket or the paper bag to take home.
- Wipe the vaginal area with toilet paper and drop the paper into the toilet.

- Put the clean panties on. Some women find this easier standing up, others sitting on the toilet. Then sit on the toilet and pull the panties up to just below the knees.
- Take the pad.
- Pull the tab off the pad and drop it in the bin. Stick the sticky side of the pad onto the panties. Press down. Positioning is important here. In a pair of panties with the gusset (crotch) sewn at both ends, the pad should be placed evenly over these sewn sections.
- Pull up panties.
- Adjust outer clothing.
- Flush toilet.
- Wash hands.

If a pad is being changed the procedure is similar. However, the used pad needs to be folded in half with the soiled side facing inwards and wrapped in toilet paper before being put in the bin. Paper bags may be easier to use than toilet paper.

You may wish to change the order of the tasks or part of the procedure, depending on the arrangements in your home, the workplace or what the woman might be likely to encounter in public toilets. If some tasks are too difficult, break them down into smaller tasks and teach them a step at a time. Remember to praise success and do not go on to the next step until you are sure the child has learnt the one before.

Another method of teaching that can be used is 'backward chaining'. This is when all the steps are done for the person except the last one, which she is taught to do. In this case it would be handwashing. When she has learnt this step you move one step backwards, and so on. If you need additional assistance, a teacher or psychologist should be able to help.

The woman will also need to be taught when to change her pad. This can be demonstrated with red food colouring or with the woman's own pads. If this is difficult for the woman to learn, pad changing can be linked to other regular activities such as meal and break times, toileting times, and bathing.

A few women have problems with appropriate behaviour at their period time. For example, they may refuse to wear the pad or take it off all the time, or tell others publicly that they have their period. To stop this, try to explain to the woman gently and patiently why the behaviour is inappropriate. Tell her what behaviour is appropriate and praise her when she achieves it. If the inappropriate behaviour persists consult a psychologist or programmer.

Some women with intellectual disability will be able to use tampons. This is fine as long as the woman remembers to change them regularly. It is best to alternate tampons with pads. A condition called toxic shock syndrome has been associated with wearing the same tampon for too long. If a woman shows any signs of fever, vomiting or diarrhoea while using tampons she should stop using them immediately and see a doctor. Wearing tampons can be an advantage if the woman likes swimming. Tampons also help a woman to learn about her body.

When a woman first gets her periods they can come at unpredictable times. Generally, however, after the first year or so a personal menstrual chart will give an idea of the pattern of a woman's periods, how long her cycle is, how many days of bleeding she can expect, how heavy her periods are likely to be, and whether she has any other symptoms associated with her periods that need to be treated. Any unusual bleeding should be investigated by a doctor.

Some women experience discomfort associated with their menstrual cycle. One form of such discomfort is the pre-menstrual syndrome. This occurs in the few days just before the period starts and symptoms include fluid retention, tender breasts, eating binges, mood swings, irritability and depression, and not doing things as well as usual.

It is often difficult for people with intellectual disability to communicate how they feel or where a pain is. This means that a woman experiencing the pre-menstrual syndrome may not be able to ask for help and may express her stress through inappropriate behaviours. If carers are not attuned to the possibility of pre-menstrual stress, they may react negatively or ignore the behaviour and since neither of these reactions will make the stress go away, the inappropriate behaviours may escalate.

Charting a woman's menstrual cycle will allow carers to see if symptoms occur regularly pre-menstrually. Some symptoms can be alleviated by medication, while others respond better to relaxation, exercise, and diet.

Some other conditions also produce symptoms which are difficult to describe but are nevertheless annoying, painful and frustrating. The most common of these are thrush, urinary tract infections and pelvic congestion. It is important to be sensitive to the possibility of these, and to seek medical attention if necessary. Naturopathic remedies can also be effective.

Some women experience period pain or cramps just before their periods begin and in the first couple of days of bleeding. Various medications can be purchased from the pharmacist to relieve this pain. Home remedies such as a hot water bottle or hot bath can also be effective. Women who are epileptic may experience more seizures around this time, and women who are incontinent may have more difficulties. In such cases it is best to consult a doctor.

Chapter 8

PERSONAL STORIES FROM PEOPLE WITH INTELLECTUAL DISABILITY

David and Narelle are boyfriend and girlfriend. They talk about their experiences growing up and establishing their independence, sexuality and relationships, and the part these have played in their lives.

What was it like for you growing up, David?

DAVID: I think I was protected really. Being the eldest I was given the benefit of the doubt. Then there was an older sister who died as a baby while Mum was having me and 'it went into me'. Then there's a brother and sister. They used to think it wasn't fair that I was the favourite. Terry is a part-time labourer and salesman — he went to 2nd or 3rd form [in high school]. I only went to 5th class [in primary school], I repeated three times. I didn't want to learn. They thought it might be best to keep me at home with Mum. They did try to put me into Morrisset [a public psychiatric and intellectual disability hospital], but I was too old to go there.

I had one friend at school, but they moved away and then I had no friends. I was very mad that my brother and sister had friends. I couldn't do sport — the brothers tried to teach me but they didn't have the extra time to give me. Only one teacher gave me extra time — I used to find I could learn when she took the time.

When I had to leave school, my parents took me for an assessment and so I stayed at home for a while. I got some part-time work — I couldn't last at full-time work. I always wanted to come home and didn't last in jobs. For five years I lived in Sydney. In my home town I was given trouble. I was always being blamed for things that happened around the district — I went to Sydney with Mum and my sister. I wanted to move out on my own when I got a good job, but Mum wouldn't let me. Dad died and we had to go back home and my problems started all over again. I couldn't last long at jobs again.

I wouldn't associate with girls — I was too shy. My parents tried to push me to have dates but I wouldn't. I was scared of people. Dad used to take me a lot to cricket and football but after a while I would get restless and want to go home. I was like that till I got to [a country town]. Then people helped to pull me out of it. Gradually I got to mingle. The people at the workshop were the most understanding of anyone I had ever met. The people there are more at my level.

I always had the feeling I was different. I always had a resentment to Mum and Dad — I couldn't understand myself. I used to be called names. There were times when I knew I didn't fit in. I would get very angry and frustrated, as if I wanted to hit out at times.

What about sex education, David? Did you get any while you were growing up?

DAVID: I didn't know anything about sex till I got to the workshop, when I was about twenty-eight or twenty-nine. I hit it off with one of the girls straight away and she invited me out and our relationship grew. She was very heavy on me sexually — she wanted to live with me. I lived with her for about twelve to eighteen months but we were having our problems — we both used to lose our tempers a lot.

Mum always hoped I would get married. I often wondered what would happen. I thought I would end up as an old bachelor.

None of the people at the workshop had any knowledge or experience of sex before they came there. I think some of the girls at the workshop couldn't look after a baby — a few could.

At some of the hostels they do everything for the residents. They don't teach them independence, and the workshop doesn't give any training. One hostel put five intellectually disabled people on a farm. They had no experience in living alone, and no training. They couldn't even cook. We see it a lot — people with no experience, no training. The guy they put in with me to share my flat — I had to make sure that he showered and took medication and I had to cook for him. It's the same with relationships — no training and no support. There should be a transition home where people can get their training.

Tell me about when you were growing up, Narelle.

NARELLE: I had problems learning at high school with maths and geography. I left at fifteen and went to work on a farm the day I left school. I had to look after the children and help the lady. I lived in. I stayed there only a couple of months. They fired me because I didn't really know how to do the housework. Then I went to help a doctor's wife while she was having a baby. I had no experience with domestic work and I burned a hole in a pair of silk pants, so I was sacked.

Then I went to the first place again and they kept me for four years. Then I went to another farm where the lady taught me a lot of things — domestic work and cooking. I was living at home and working a couple of days a week. I was there for eight and a half years. They took a lot of care with me — they knew I was only slow.

Mum brought me up strictly because she wanted me to be a good girl. She was very protective — if I was still at home she would still be buying clothes for me. I used to talk to her about getting married but she never liked me talking to boys. I wasn't interested in boys really, but Ian was a nice gentleman. He was actually the same way I was — his parents protected him too. He came to my 21st birthday party. Ian was engaged to my girlfriend then. She left him. I liked him but his parents really used to sit on him. Though just having him as a friend helped me to come out. I was too shy then. I used to go with him without Mum and Dad knowing about it. We never had sex. We helped each other out really. I was still frightened out of my brain. Mum used to warn me against boys. She'd mention that boys can give you children, and say, don't get into trouble. I had only seen little boys running around without clothes and I didn't know they grew. When I had that experience I was frightened.

Narelle, did you get any other sex education while you were growing up?

NARELLE: My periods started when I was eleven years old. Mum never told me that girls get periods. I started getting sick when I was at school and when I got home I had blood on my pants. Then Mum just told me that all girls get that.

I had to do everything that Mum wanted and I'm getting to the stage where I want to do what I want [thirty-four].

I left home when I was twenty-nine years old. I had a lot of pressure from my parents not to leave — I wanted to get married. I asked the doctor if I could get married because I had met a nice young man I wanted to marry. I didn't know anything about sex until I left home and my girlfriend and her boyfriend decided to teach me. They took me to their flat and . . . he sat me on his knees and he had nothing on at all. He asked me to take my clothes off, but I didn't — I didn't want to have anything to do with boys at all.

The boys at school touched me in the private area — touched me here. I didn't know what they were doing — and why they were calling me bad names — because I didn't know anything about sex. Even when I was in primary school the boys got me that way, when I was seven or eight years old.

When I first left home I stayed with a woman I knew from town. Then I shared a flat with someone else I couldn't get on with.

I wasn't really prepared for living and sharing with someone else — twenty-nine is too old to leave your parents. They just saw me as living with them as long as they lived and they made provision in their wills that this couple, their friends, would look after me. They really didn't think I could look after myself. It was Dad who told me that I was a bit retarded and I resented him for that all along.

I didn't know I could leave home — the community sister gave me the idea I could go to this workshop. I met David straight away there. We were attracted to each other right from the start.

Mum didn't really let me grow up. She didn't expect me to do anything well. I found life hard because I knew I was slow, and people laughed at me.

The doctor explained to us why we couldn't have a baby — that the baby would come out too small and that I would have a miscarriage.

Mum didn't take our engagement very well. She gave me a good talking to. She tried to make rules for my life even when I left home. She told David he shouldn't be visiting past seven o'clock.

I thought I'd be home with Mum and Dad for the rest of my life. The expectations of me were low and ground me down. I never had the feeling that I could do anything.

I would have wanted a baby — I wanted to get married and have a little baby. But the doctor told me that I could have a baby but it could end up retarded or have something wrong with it. And I have to think of David too. When you love somebody, you've got to give and take and David didn't want one.

DAVID: Mum and the doctor said there was a big possibility that I could have a baby that was deformed or retarded. And knowing what I had to go through I decided I could not risk that.

Robert and Julie, two parents with intellectual disability, talk about their marriage and their baby.

How did you get together?

JULIE: We became friends after meeting at a Self Advocacy Conference in 1986, but in 1989 I realised that I really had a crush on Robert. I waited to be sure for a few months and when it was clear that Robert wouldn't ever make the first move I did. In August of 1990 we made a long-term commitment to each other with plans to get married in 1992. All that changed of course when I found out I was pregnant.

Did you plan the pregnancy?

ROBERT: No. When we first suspected Julie was pregnant we sat down and discussed what we would do if she was. We knew that there would probably be a lot of pressure to give up the baby and that we should make a decision before everybody else started to add their expert advice. We realised that we were quite excited at the idea of having a baby and decided we would keep it and bring forward the date of the wedding.

What were other people's reactions?

ROBERT: Pretty much as we expected. Even our main support people tried to talk us into an abortion. Many people didn't say to our faces that they thought we wouldn't cope but you could tell what they were thinking. You develop a sixth sense when you live in an institution. Our families were supportive and our close friends were all for it.

How did you prepare for the baby?

ROBERT: We applied for a two bedroom Housing Department flat instead of the one bedroom we were in. They wouldn't give it to us until after the baby was born so this caused us anxiety and made us feel not at all prepared. We both attended prenatal classes at the hospital. We had a support person to help us do the things we needed to do. Julie kept working right up until the birth and was very calm about it all until she went into labour.

How were the first few weeks?

JULIE: I wanted to try breastfeeding but it wasn't for me. I'm happy with the decision I made now as we can both feed her. Amanda-Lee had to stay in hospital until she weighed five pounds, so I came out before her. I was pretty depressed in the first three weeks but that's normal.

ROBERT: We were advised to go to Tresillian [a facility providing assistance to mothers with new babies] for the first week. We both went and lived in and they taught us all the things we needed to know such as getting into feeding routines and what to do when she cried and how to bath her and change nappies [diapers].

Did you get any extra support because you were disabled?

JULIE: We had a community nurse come to visit us once a week in our home for eight weeks. Now we go to the regular Community Health Centre. We also attended parenting classes at Family Planning. They were very good classes and we wish we had kept them up longer.

Where does your support come from now?

ROBERT: Our auntie is very supportive and does a lot of babysitting. We also have a friend who has a two-year-old and gives us tips. Our support is mainly from our family and friends which we are very lucky to have. We both really enjoy parenthood despite it being very hard sometimes.

How do you find people's attitudes now?

ROBERT: People's attitudes have really changed now they see how well we are coping. You just have to show people that you can do it. We're both proud of ourselves and of our baby.

Chapter 9
SOCIAL LIFE

Everyone needs the pleasure that comes from making friends and socialising. Friends should include people of both sexes. There is no reason why people with intellectual disability should not be encouraged to lead a life that is as full as possible, and this means learning the social skills which will help them to develop friendships. The more social skills children with intellectual disability learn, the easier it will be for them to relate to other people and the better they will feel about themselves. Children who relate only to their family will lead very limited lives.

Parents and other carers should help to create social opportunities. Encourage school-age children to bring their friends home after school. Perhaps you could organise with another family to take turns at weekend outings, so that you are sometimes relieved of the responsibility. Get in touch with groups which organise recreation programs and camps for people with disabilities, as these activities will provide opportunities for your children to participate more fully in their community.

Some parents reading this may feel overwhelmed by the responsibility of acting as social facilitators for their children. It is true that parents whose children have special needs have a harder task in this sphere than most parents. That is why it is important to join or form a group so that you are not alone.

Respite care is one way that children and young people with intellectual disability can begin learning how to live away from home with people other than their immediate family. Even a day spent in respite care or a sleepover one weekend a month, can be beneficial, for both child and parents.

When planning social activities for your child with intellectual disability, think in terms of what your other children or your friends' children do. They may enjoy a slumber party, a special afternoon tea, dinner at a friend's house, or going shopping with a friend. Such activities do not have to be expensive or elaborate, but they need to be frequent, so that acquired skills can be consolidated.

Learning how to use a telephone can be a very useful skill for conducting a social life. It can also be very important in an emergency or when help is needed. One mother we know bought a medical bleeper system so that she could keep in touch with her child.

A very useful way to help children to learn social skills is to involve them in role-play at home. Select a situation and let the family members act it out. For example, going shopping, or riding home on the bus.

When constructing these situations, remember that you are teaching your child significant survival skills. For example, you could act out a situation in which a child is accosted on the school bus by somebody making an improper remark. Ask the children to say and show how they would react.

Instructions can be simple. For example: 'Peter is the stranger who gets on the bus. Mary is riding on the bus. Peter, sit next to Mary, start to talk to her and put your arm around her. Mary, you tell us what you are going to say to this stranger.'

This kind of role-play is valuable for all members of the family as it prompts everyone to review and clarify their values. In this example, you might discuss the following question: 'Should strangers put their arms around girls they don't know? Is it rude to ignore a stranger who is so friendly? If the stranger is really nice and says he knows your brother, should you get off the bus with him? If you are feeling scared and in need of help, who would you turn to?'

Construct other role-plays. Other family members can volunteer situations which they would like to act out; often these will be actual experiences which they did not know how to handle at the time. Of course learning to handle such situations does not eliminate the risk, but it may lessen the chances of an unpleasant outcome.

Young people with intellectual disability need opportunities to explore their community and to exercise their independence. Certain precautions can help to minimise the risks involved. Make sure they always carry some form of identification, for example, a bracelet or a watch with your phone number or some kind of identification tag, or perhaps a necklace with an identity disc. Perhaps you could give your child a wallet or purse, with the exact money required for a public phone call, along with a short list of phone numbers they could use in a crisis. A phone card may be easier to use than coins.

Like everyone else, people with intellectual disability do not stop growing and learning when they stop going to school or living with their families. In fact, one could say that some of the most important learning about 'life' takes place when we are young adults. It is then that we learn how to survive in the world without the protection of our parents, and how to interact with a variety of people in a variety of social situations.

Parents whose young adult children are still living at home need to find ways to help their children conduct an independent social life. If the young adult moves into a community-based home, then this becomes the responsibility of the residential care worker.

Residential care staff can be very creative in providing opportunities for social experiences. Outings such as shopping, going to restaurants, horse-riding and bowling are not really enough, particularly if these activities are only done with residents of the same house. It is important to find ways to involve individuals from the community in the lives of residents, in order to widen their circle of friends. Churches, business clubs and citizen advocacy services are some of the options that can be explored.

Extending social skills can be done through parlour games such as charades, role-playing daily interactions or scheduling conversation times with suggested conversational topics. Card games and games to enhance self-esteem and mutual trust can also be scheduled into the weekly routine. Dinners and parties, with all that such events involve, from invitations to cooking to making sure that guests are happy, can be very important. Even reinforcing such basic interactions as saying 'good morning' to each other or 'hi, how was your day' when people come home from work, can add to the mutual respect and sense of being valued which people give one another.

Not all people with intellectual disability have language and of those who do not all have the same level of language skills. But even those without language can learn to express themselves and develop some level of social interaction. Methods of communication include signing, the use of pictorial symbols, photographs, the written word, and a mixture of these.

It is crucial that children with intellectual disability are taught the medium of communication most appropriate for them from an early age, and that this is used consistently across all settings, throughout their lives. Without some form of communication, there is no possibility of social interaction, and without social interaction quality of life is minimal. Taking part in community activities, not as passive onlookers but as active participants, is the only way to maintain and enhance communication and social skills.

Dating

At some point during adolescence or young adulthood your son or daughter may develop an interest in someone of the opposite sex. This is a normal part of growing up. The social skills appropriate to dating can be taught by the same methods used to teach other social skills.

It is a good idea to prepare for this eventuality early, preferably before your child reaches puberty. You and another parent could organise an outing for a small mixed sex group of children. Then you could try inviting one of your child's classmates or friends of the opposite sex and take them both on an outing. In these situations, you, the parent, will provide the appropriate role modelling. For example, you could take your son and a girl classmate out to a movie or MacDonald's, and prompt your son through the appropriate social steps.

This social interaction can then be reinforced through discussions and role-plays at home and in class. At these times other issues, such as 'petting', may come up.

The issue of petting is a difficult one. Parents in general may be able to accept that holding hands, even kissing and cuddling are inevitable. The problem is knowing when to stop. Here is one way to approach the subject of petting:

'When two people (a boy and a girl) like each other very much, they might want to hold hands and cuddle and kiss. Sometimes that makes them feel so good and 'sexy', that they want to touch each other all over. A boy might then get an erection, and a girl's vagina might feel moist. At this point it is best to stop and not go on touching each other, as it could lead to sexual intercourse. Sexual intercourse is not something you do when out on a date unless you and your friend love each other very much and want to be together all the time. Also, there are a lot of things you and your friend need to talk about, with each other and with your parents (or other carers), before you decide to have sex. Most people, especially when they are your age, just like to kiss and cuddle when they are out together.'

This discussion should also cover issues such as mutual consent and safe sex.

Loneliness can lead to a lowering of self-esteem and to depression. Being able to make friends and relate to other people are important aspects of growing up for everyone and we have to help people with intellectual disability learn the relevant social skills. They also need opportunities to practise these skills in familiar settings with their families before moving out into the community. If they are properly prepared they will then be able to make friends and have an interesting and varied social life in the community.

Chapter 10
MARRIAGE

Two people in their forties, both of whom had been living in an institution for people with epilepsy for many years, asked for permission to marry. The doctor told them that they could get married, but that they were not allowed to have sex.

The mother of a twenty-six-year-old woman with intellectual disability was practically in tears as she told her story. Her daughter wanted to marry a forty-year-old man who worked in the same workshop, but the man's father would not consent to the marriage unless the woman underwent a tubal ligation. The woman's mother wanted the marriage to go ahead because she felt that her daughter had a good relationship, but she was unwilling to encourage her daughter to have a tubal ligation.

Given that marriage is seen by the community at large as a valued and normal part of life, it is not surprising that many couples with intellectual disability wish to marry. A good marriage can considerably enhance a person's quality of life.

In Australia and the United Kingdom, couples with intellectual disability are legally allowed to marry, as long as they are of age and can demonstrate an understanding of the marriage contract. In the United States, in some states, couples with intellectual disability are not legally allowed to marry. However, the laws prohibiting such marriages are not always enforced. Advocacy groups are campaigning to have these laws changed. They argue that the right to marry is fundamental and that data shows that people with intellectual disability are no less successful as spouses than non-disabled people. In fact, given people's recent successes in community living and open employment, it is reasonable to assume that many people who were previously thought to be incapable of meeting the demands of marriage, may well be able to meet its challenges.

Married couples with intellectual disability, although they often live in sub-standard housing with little money, generally indicate satisfaction with their marriage, particularly in terms of the sense of companionship marriage provides.

Some couples may need specific skills and support to enhance the possibilities of their marriage succeeding. Communication skills and education on relationships, sexuality, contraception and child-rearing choices will all be important. Training in communication skills enables people to resolve conflict more easily when it arises in their relationship. Education on relationships and sexuality can help partners to identify their expectations in the relationship and realistic goals. Education on contraception and child-rearing choices enables a couple to consider the changes that occur in marital relationships when couples have children, whether this is desired in their relationship, and other responsibilities of parenting.

Domestic duties and money management skills will also be needed if the couple is to live independently as a unit. Housing alternatives may need to be explored if the current accommodation is not suitable for a married couple. Relationships with relatives, especially if they do not support the marriage, may be a primary issue, particularly if these relatives are normally a source of support. All these issues need to be discussed before a wedding takes place.

Couples also need to be aware of their local community resources. Some couples may need specific forms of support, but even where they do not, activities and friendship networks in the community are still very important. Generally speaking, the success of marriages between people with intellectual disability is subject to the same factors as any other marriage. These factors include partners choosing each other rather than parents making the choice, not marrying too young, having sufficient income to provide for needs, being emotionally stable, having role models of good marriage in the family, and the absence of substantial family opposition to the marriage.

It may well be that some people with intellectual disability develop a more realistic view of the joys and demands of marriage than many non-disabled people who do not explore these issues as thoroughly.

Chapter 11
SEX WITHOUT MARRIAGE

Although more and more parents are coming to terms with their children forming de facto relationships, many still feel anxious about children with intellectual disability forming such relationships. They repress such relationships between their children with intellectual disability because since they, the parents, have decided that marriage is out of the question, it follows that sex must be too.

On the other hand, some parents and disability workers condone sex without marriage between people with intellectual disability because they feel that such people are not capable of marriage.

In this context it is important to remember that not all sensual relationships involve sex. Some intimate relationships may only involve hugging, kissing, holding hands and sharing experiences, in a manner which is very important to the people concerned. Sexual intercourse may not be part of the agenda and marriage may not be relevant. Try to stay in touch with the couple's relationship without being intrusive, so that if sex is likely to occur, they will be adequately prepared for it, especially with regard to contraception and avoiding sexually transmitted diseases and AIDS. And if the couple wish to marry, investigate this option as it arises.

Of course, regardless of whether a couple wishes to have sex, marry or live in a de facto relationship, they can still benefit from learning skills in communication, and forming and maintaining relationships.

Sometimes a couple or an individual will need assistance in their sexual relationships, as do others in the community. This may be because they have a sexual dysfunction, such as the male ejaculating too quickly, or because they do not know what to do to help their partner enjoy the experience. If this is the case, education can be helpful. The parent or worker could explain that when people have sex they like to be kissed and cuddled, and have various parts of their bodies, including their private parts, touched. These are important and enjoyable parts of having sex. It may be necessary to explain that the man can sometimes put his penis into the woman's

50

vagina, and move it in and out. Or the man can suck the woman's vagina or the woman suck the man's penis. These are all things that people can do when they are having sex.

Of course it is important to emphasise that people should only have sex when they want to, and with a person of their choice. And they should only do what makes them feel comfortable. It is also necessary to explain the importance of safe sex to avoid sexually transmitted diseases and AIDS. No semen, vaginal fluid or blood should enter the other person's body. Kissing, cuddling and touching are safe. People should use condoms when having vaginal, oral or anal sex in order to prevent infection. Safe sex is covered in more detail in Chapter 14.

Sometimes a person with sexual difficulties does not require education but has a sexual dysfunction which only a trained sexual counsellor will be able to deal with. Your local doctor, Family Planning Association or Planned Parenthood Federation will be able to make an appropriate referral.

We know that sex without marriage strains the moral standards of many parents and staff, and we are not suggesting that you abandon your standards. But if you do accept sex without marriage in non-disabled couples, it may be appropriate to reconsider your position with regard to couples with intellectual disability. Such couples may not wish to marry or may not be able to marry. Sex is an important part of life and an energising life force — there is no reason why people with intellectual disability should be denied it.

Chapter 12
CHILDREN

A woman with intellectual disability has just become pregnant with her fourth child. Her previous three children were removed by the Court because they were neglected. No one has ever educated her about parenting or contraception or counselled her over the loss of her three children. Her doctor wants to perform an abortion and sterilisation.

Although many parents and carers feel positive about people with intellectual disability having relationships and marrying, they often feel that such couples should not have children and advocate the long-term use of contraception.

One of the main concerns expressed is that couples with intellectual disability may have children with a similar disability. In fact, for most people with intellectual disability this is not the case, and their chances of having a child with intellectual disability are the same as for the rest of the population. If parenting is being considered it is recommended that genetic evaluation and counselling take place. This will tell the parents if their respective disabilities can be passed on genetically, and what the chances are of this happening.

The other primary concern is whether parents with intellectual disability, and particularly the mother who is usually the primary carer, will be able to care adequately for the child.

The demands of parenthood are variable and unpredictable. Initially they involve dealing with the changes of pregnancy and then childbirth. In early childhood the responsibilities of parenthood include total care of the child — food preparation, bathing and dressing, detecting signs of illness and responding to them appropriately, and knowing how to stimulate the child. As children grow older the demands change. However, the basic needs of children always remain the same: unconditional love, attention, safety, and the opportunity to develop self-help skills.

52

In the past there has been little research on the ability of parents with intellectual disability to raise children successfully. However, in recent times, various agencies have undertaken to train parents with intellectual disability in parenting skills and provide them with support.

From such work it has become clear that some couples with intellectual disability can meet the responsibilities of parenting a child, especially if community services are available to provide training and additional support when required. However, it is equally clear that some people with intellectual disability cannot acquire the skills necessary to parent adequately.

Unfortunately, in our society, marriage and parenting are often seen in tandem. Social conditioning concerning this is very strong and is reinforced on television, in magazines, by neighbours, families and carers. However, marriage and parenting need to be seen as separate issues and separate choices.

Parents and carers may need to point out to a child with intellectual disability that not all couples choose to have children, and that this is not an indication of failure in life. Point out role models of couples who have chosen not to have children and who are happy with this decision. Be careful not to revere pregnant friends.

Arrange for the person with intellectual disability to spend some time around babies and, if possible, be responsible for some of their care. This could be done with relatives or at a local child care centre. This will show the person that babies, although they are sometimes smiling, sweet and cuddly, can also be difficult, noisy and messy, and that they never go away. Teach them about the economic realities of having a child or children, about the work involved and the pressures on social life. Use other parents as examples or relate it to their own lives.

Some educators arrange for the person with intellectual disability to care for a pet in order to illustrate some of the constant responsibilities involved in caring for a child.

People with intellectual disability also need to understand that the birth of a child brings additional pressures to a relationship. They need to understand that if a child is neglected or abused he or she can be removed by social service agencies and ultimately by a Court. There are also legal restrictions in some American states on people with intellectual disability having children. This is not the case in Australia or the United Kingdom, and international treaties recognise the right of all people to decide whether or not to have children.

Education about the realities of parenting, and the options involved, is important because without sufficient information people with intellectual disability are not in a position to make a realistic decision concerning their parenting capabilities. The emotional aspects of this decision also need to be taken into account. Of those who have made the decision not to parent some feel positive about their decision and others feel a sense of regret.

It is always better if such education takes place before a pregnancy occurs, because the pregnancy can add emotional factors which cloud the important issues.

If a couple or a woman decides to have a child, ensure that they have access to appropriate community services. The woman may benefit from prenatal or birth classes run by the local hospital. Find out about baby health centres, child development services, and child care centres. Find out whether there are local agencies running parenting training classes for people with intellectual disability.

Parenting training classes usually include information and development of skills in the following areas: children's basic needs and child development, parent/child interaction, daily routines, time concepts and medical care. Some even cover making toys. These classes are generally run for parents with mild or moderate intellectual disability.

Chapter 13
HOMOSEXUALITY

Homosexuality continues to be one of society's sexual taboos. We still hear people referring to it as a perversion or as some sort of illness. However, these notions have been consistently challenged in the past few years, and although it is not possible to generalise about the attitudes of therapists and other health professionals, it is true to say that most professional people no longer consider homosexuality as an illness which requires a cure, and you will no longer find it listed as an illness in books on medicine or psychiatry.

Many religious groups now have their own gay groups and most major denominations have at least had discussions about the issue of homosexuality over the past ten years. Generally, the attitudes of most religious groups have become increasingly liberal.

Homosexual acts between consenting adults are legal in some Australian and American states and in the United Kingdom. You will need to check what the situation is in your state. In fact, in Australia it is an offence to discriminate against people who are homosexual in most areas of employment, accommodation and services.

The basic problem with homosexuality is not the behaviour itself, but the persecution of or discrimination against the person who is homosexual. No one has ever been able to demonstrate that sexual stimulation of or by a person of one's own sex is intrinsically harmful. And in any case homosexual practices are also practised by heterosexuals.

The determinants of sexual orientation are not known. Some people believe that homosexuality is caused by genetic, chromosomal or hormonal factors. Others regard environment and relationships with parents as more significant. At the moment there is no convincing evidence either way.

There is a distinction to be drawn here between sexual activity and sexual orientation. In single sex institutions, such as prisons and some institutions for people with intellectual disability, it is impossible for people to have sex unless they have it with people of the same sex or by masturbating. So having sex with people of the same sex does not always mean that a person is homosexual. Of course this can be very confusing for some people with intellectual disability.

Let us consider some simple ways of explaining differences in sexual preference to people with intellectual disability. 'Homosexuals are men who prefer to have sex with men, or women who prefer to have sex with women. A person who likes to have sex with both men and women is called bisexual. Heterosexuals are men who like to have sex with women and women who like to have sex with men. Another word for homosexual men and women is gay. Sometimes homosexual women are called lesbians. It is not okay to use other words like poofter or queer, because it is like swearing at people.'

People with intellectual disability who are homosexual may have additional problems in asserting and enjoying their sexuality, because of the attitudes of those around them. It is vital that parents and staff do not overreact to people having homosexual sex or homosexual relationships because this can cause guilt and fear. Provided there is no exploitation, and provided they are having safe sex, no harm can come of it.

If the rest of the community is permitted by law to take part in homosexual activity, there is no reason why people with intellectual disability should not have the same rights. The range of people who are homosexual is as variable as the range of those who are heterosexual.

The main problem that could arise in this area is exploitation. Men and boys, disabled and non-disabled, may be approached in public toilets or in the institutions where they live. Parents and staff have a responsibility to explain that this could happen and to teach ways of handling it. This can be done by role-playing. Also, make sure that the boy or man with intellectual disability urinates in the same way as other men so that he does not draw attention to himself. He should not drop his pants when he urinates. If he does, show him the pants up method. The reward is the sense of security that comes from acting like other people.

Sometimes workers who care for people with intellectual disability in institutions decide to adopt a permissive attitude towards homosexual acts, but only within the institution. They do this because there is no danger of pregnancy and because they accept the need for physical contact. However, it is distressing to see the same staff reprimanding these people for displaying such affection, for example holding hands, when out in the community. It can be difficult for people with intellectual disability to understand the difference between what is acceptable in the institution and what is acceptable in the community.

People with intellectual disability should have the opportunity to mix with people of both the same and the opposite sex, to experience the range of relationships available to others in the community, and to more ably determine their own sexual preferences. They need to know about homosexuality as well as about heterosexuality, and if they are homosexual they need to know where it is safe to be physically affectionate with their partner. If you feel that you don't have sufficient information to do this effectively, contact a local or national gay organisation.

People with disability often ask questions in groups when we are talking about homosexuality. One of the most common questions is: 'How do homosexuals have sex?' So we explain what people might do, just as we do when people ask us questions about heterosexual sex. 'They kiss, cuddle and touch different parts of each other's bodies, including the private parts. One man can suck the penis of the other man, or put his penis in the other man's anus. Or he can rub the other man's penis with his hand. Women also kiss, cuddle and touch, including each other's breasts and vulva, with their hands and mouth.' At all times we emphasise the importance of safe sex to avoid sexually transmitted diseases. No semen, vaginal fluid or blood should enter the other person's body. Kissing, cuddling and touching are safe. People should use condoms or dental dams when having vaginal, oral or anal sex in order to prevent infection. Safe sex is covered in more detail in Chapter 14.

We provide this explicit information because we believe that people with intellectual disability have the right to be safe and to have the same choices as others in the community. However, we acknowledge that some people in the community may not agree with our views.

Chapter 14
BEING SEXUALLY HEALTHY

Good sexual health can contribute to general self-esteem and a sense of well-being. Poor sexual health can lead to pain, illness and even death. Fortunately, good sexual health mainly involves preventive measures which are easy to implement.

To maintain good sexual health people with intellectual disability need to be taught the importance of regular checkups, how to recognise when something is wrong and where to go for treatment if this is the case.

Breast Checks

Breast cancer is one of the most common forms of cancer in Western women. Fortunately, most breast problems are not cancer. However, if a woman does have a breast cancer, the earlier it is detected, the greater the chances of cure.

Breast self-examination is the first step in detecting breast problems. Women are shown how to look for changes or unusual lumps and they then check their breasts at home once a month. Some women with intellectual disability will be able to learn to examine their breasts in this way. However, other women with intellectual disability will not possess the judgement to be able to perform this self-examination thoroughly and will therefore need to have annual breast examinations by their doctor or at a Family Planning or Planned Parenthood centre. It is also wise for women who examine their own breasts to have occasional checks by a doctor.

Some women are at a higher risk of breast cancer and they should be more closely monitored. These include women whose mothers or sisters have had breast cancer, women who have not had children and women who had children late in their reproductive years.

Pap Tests

The pap test involves taking cells from the cervix or mouth of the uterus to detect changes that may become cancerous. Changes in

58

these cells can happen for other reasons such as because the woman has an infection. But if the changes are detected early treatment can be instituted before the woman gets cancer.

The causes of cervical cancer are not known, although it is thought that intercourse at an early age and multiple partners may increase the chances of getting it. Others think that it may be caused by a virus.

Certainly all women should have regular pap tests from the time of their first sexual experience or from their mid-twenties. A woman with no previous abnormal results should have a pap test at least once every two years. Some doctors recommend yearly pap tests.

Before a woman has a pap test it is essential that she understands exactly what is involved in a pelvic examination. It may take several clinic visits before she feels comfortable about having it done.

Testes Checks

Cancer of the testes is the most common cancer found in men between the ages of fifteen and thirty-five. Its cause is unknown, but like most cancers early diagnosis and treatment is vital. With early detection and treatment there is an almost 100 per cent cure rate for this type of cancer.

Testicular self-examination to detect any changes or unusual lumps can be taught to men who then examine their testes at home once a month, in much the same way as women examine their breasts. As with breast problems, some changes will not be cancerous. Some men with intellectual disability may not have the judgement to perform the check thoroughly or detect changes, and so will need to be examined annually by their doctor.

Sexually Transmitted Diseases

Sexually transmitted diseases are diseases which are transmitted through intercourse or oral sex. Contrary to what some people believe they cannot be caught from toilet seats, door knobs or swimming pools. They can only be caught by having sex with someone who already has the infection.

Gonorrhea and syphilis are the most widely known. Both are very contagious but they are easy to diagnose and treat. Non-specific urethritis (NSU) is a very common STD, mainly diagnosed in men. Herpes is a fairly common STD in both men and women and although very painful, an attack will eventually subside without treatment.

There are a number of other STDs and it may be worth consulting other sources for details of these and the STDs already mentioned. See the Resources section at the end of the book.

There are several ways of reducing the risk of catching a sexually transmitted disease. First, do not have sexual intercourse. This is the best and only method if no condoms are available. Second, always use a condom when having vaginal, oral or anal sex. Third, maintain a monogamous relationship with one partner who is uninfected with any sexually transmitted disease, including AIDS. Remember that the more partners a person has the higher the risk of encountering a sexually transmitted disease.

People with intellectual disability should be taught to recognise the following symptoms in themselves and to seek medical attention if they occur: any unusual discharge from the penis or vagina; pain on urination; sores on or around the penis or vagina; itchiness in the genital area; a rash which is not itchy especially if it is on the palms of the hands or the soles of the feet. Some STDs have no obvious symptoms but if left untreated can have very serious effects in the long term. So if a person finds out that a partner has an STD he or she should always go for a checkup. For the same reason, if people find out that they have an STD they should always tell all their sexual partners so that they can go and be treated too.

HIV and AIDS

The letters HIV stand for Human Immunodeficiency Virus. This is a virus which progressively destroys the body's natural ability to fight off other infections. The letters AIDS stand for Acquired Immune Deficiency Syndrome. This is the fatal disease which is the end result of the stages of infection with HIV.

Many people still have a strong emotional fear of AIDS and HIV, which has resulted in widespread irrational discrimination against infected people. This is largely due to misleading media reports and the many myths about how the virus is transmitted. The following should dispel some of these myths.

HIV is found in the blood, semen and vaginal fluids of people who are infected. Anyone who has the virus can pass it on to someone else through these fluids, and that person in turn can become infected with HIV. However, the infected fluids must enter the bloodstream of the uninfected person. This is most likely to happen in three ways: during anal or vaginal sex, when people are sharing used needles and syringes, or to a baby during pregnancy or labour. In Australia, the United Kingdom and the United States it can no longer be passed on in a blood transfusion as the blood supplies in these countries are now safe.

As with other STDs, the use of a condom can reduce the risk of transmission, and sex without penetration virtually eliminates the risk of infection altogether.

Once infected with HIV, a person is infected for life and can pass the infection on. A blood test can detect the presence of HIV. Once a person is known to be HIV positive, there are a number of treatments available which can help to slow down the progress of the disease.

A person with intellectual disability cannot be tested for HIV unless he or she, or a legally designated other person, gives an informed consent. An informed consent for a test for HIV means the person must understand the potential positive and negative consequences of the test being done. Positive consequences (apart from a negative result) include being able to use treatments which could slow the progress of the disease and being aware of the importance of practising safe sex so as not to pass the virus on. Negative consequences include the possibility of being discriminated against, especially in obtaining employment or accommodation.

Unfortunately there are already some people with intellectual disability in Western countries who have died from AIDS and others who are HIV infected.

Vaginal Infections

There are some infections which a woman can get which are not sexually transmitted. These include monilia and thrush. Many bacteria normally grow in a woman's vagina but sometimes an infection can occur which needs treatment. A woman is more likely to have one of these infections if she is run down, on the contraceptive pill or antibiotics or wears tight nylon panties. Symptoms may include itchiness, soreness, abnormal discharge or frequent urination.

Safe Sex

Safe sex refers to the practice of taking certain precautions to avoid unwanted pregnancy and passing on or being infected by a sexually transmitted disease or AIDS. To be completely safe no semen, vaginal fluid or blood should enter the other person's body. Kissing, cuddling and touching are safe but when having vaginal, oral or anal sex, a condom should always be worn.

It is advisable to have regular medical checkups, especially if sex is occurring with more than one person. If a couple are contemplating sex for the first time, it may be wise for both to have a checkup and an AIDS test first. In the meantime it is essential to use condoms.

In this regard condoms must be freely and easily available, especially to people with intellectual disability. This is the responsibility of the parents or disability workers. Remember that the purpose of condoms is not only to avoid unwanted pregnancy, and they should be worn even when another form of contraception is being used.

The subject of contraception is discussed in Chapter 15.

Chapter 15
FERTILITY ISSUES

A twenty-year-old woman who had had three abortions, was still without contraception and had no understanding of her sexuality. She was living with her boyfriend and working in a sheltered workshop.

'The ball of responsibility gets thrown from one court to another — parent, professional, sheltered workshop, government department — and often gets dropped by everyone like a hot potato.'

Parent of a thirty-six-year-old man who lives in an institution

'I was very scared of getting pregnant and of having sex — anyone touching me.'

Joanne

Contraception and parenthood for people with intellectual disability are areas of serious concern for many parents and workers.

More and more people with intellectual disability are living in the community and leading independent lives. In doing so they observe their siblings, their friends and their neighbours having relationships, marrying and having children as a matter of course, and this leads them to expect the same rights to love, have sex, marry and have children.

It is important therefore to include in any sex education program information about the sorts of relationships people can have and the responsibilities involved in these relationships, both to partners and any possible children. In this regard, information about contraception is vital and it should be given to both males and females as this is a responsibility which should be shared.

Sex education is the responsibility of both disability workers and parents and it needs to be clear and positive. Trying to prevent a woman from becoming pregnant by making her afraid of sex, by telling her she can never get married, or by keeping her ignorant about what sex is, is not only unethical, but likely to be ineffective.

Instilling a fear or distaste for sex in someone can also deprive that person of the opportunity to form healthy, caring and mutually supportive relationships. A mother of a thirty-six-year-old man speaks regretfully of her son's loneliness. Apparently he refuses to even hold hands with a woman because that is sex and sex is dirty.

Winifred Kempton tells the story of a school student who returned to the classroom after her lunch break looking very dishevelled. Upon questioning the girl, her teacher discovered that she had been having sex with one of the boys in the bushes. However the girl did not realise what she had been doing because her mother had only told her never to let a boy kiss her or touch her legs, and neither of these things had happened.

Contraception is often seen as being important by families and staff for women with intellectual disability because of the possibility of rape. While this is certainly an issue, it is not the primary one in sexual assault. Women should, as far as possible, be taught skills to minimise the possibility of sexual assault. Of course, it is not possible to protect a woman, disabled or not, against all possibility of sexual assault.

Where sexual activity is occurring, or is likely to occur, contraception will be necessary, either some or all of the time. Family Planning Associations and Planned Parenthood Federations and educators can be helpful in providing accurate information about contraception to people with intellectual disability, their families and staff. Families or staff can later go over the information with the person at home. If the person is a minor then teachers or health professionals will need to discuss it with the parents or carers. Of course, if the person is an adult the issue should be discussed with him or her and preferably the partner as well.

Some questions that may need to be answered are:

- How much can the person or couple understand?
- Does the person and the partner know the basic facts about sexual intercourse?
- Do they know how pregnancy occurs?
- Do they know what contraception is?
- What resources are there to help educate the person or couple?

- Is contraception needed?
- Can the person give his or her medical history?
- How much say does the advocate or guardian have in the decision-making process?

Every attempt should be made to inform the person or couple, even if this takes several sessions. The person or couple will also need to be prepared for what will happen in a doctor's visit. For example, if the woman needs to have a pelvic examination, this must be described beforehand, and several visits to the clinic may be required before she feels comfortable about having the procedure done.

There are many different forms of contraception available. No one method is suitable for all people with intellectual disability. For each individual each method will need to be evaluated in terms of the person's health, motivation, skills to use a particular method reliably, and the effectiveness of the method in preventing pregnancy.

Several available methods of contraception are not included in this chapter. These are the natural methods such as the rhythm method, the Billings or mucous method, the basal temperature method, withdrawal, and also barrier methods such as diaphragms, contraceptive sponges and spermicides. This is because these methods can require sophisticated calculations, careful judgement, a high level of partner co-operation and considerable manual dexterity. Many non-disabled people find these methods difficult to use effectively.

If, after every effort has been made, the person is still unable to make an informed decision, then another appropriate person will need to authorise it. Depending on the laws in your state this will either be a parent, a legally appointed guardian or the head of a service.

The Condom

Condoms have become an important method of contraception because of their additional advantage of providing significant protection against most sexually transmitted diseases and AIDS.

The condom is a rubber sheath that is placed over the erect penis before intercourse takes place. It is an effective contraceptive, provided it is used properly. This means that both the man and woman need to know when and how to put it on and take it off. The best way to learn this is by practising it over and over again on a model. Your local Family Planning Association or Planned Parenthood Federation may have instructors who can assist with this training. It is also necessary to make sure that the couple know where and how to buy condoms. Check that the local pharmacist or supermarket will be understanding and helpful with your clients. It may be a good idea to keep a supply of condoms in the house or community residence.

If training is successful, and if the man is well-motivated to avoid pregnancy and sexually transmitted disease, then condoms can be an extremely reliable form of contraception.

What are the advantages of condoms?

- Protection against sexually transmitted diseases and unwanted pregnancy.

What are the disadvantages of condoms?

- Expense, depending on how often sex takes place.
- Failure to use them properly.
- Embarrassment at having to put them on during the sex act.

The Pill

The oral contraceptive pill is an effective method of contraception provided it is taken daily, preferably at around the same time. However, it does have side effects.

The ability of women with intellectual disability to use the pill successfully varies and is not always dependent on their level of disability. If the woman is supervised there should be no problems with pill-taking. If the woman has problems remembering to take the pill, taking it can be tied to some other regular daily activity, such as showering. However, other factors can interfere with effective use of the pill, particularly if the woman wants to have a baby.

Some of the more important factors associated with taking the pill are summarised in the following.

What are the advantages of the pill?

- It is very reliable if taken correctly.
- No discomfort or pain is associated with its use.
- Frequent pelvic examinations are not necessary.
- It is separate from the sex act.
- It involves a pill-taking routine with which the woman may already be familiar.

- It will probably reduce menstrual flow and period pains and possibly pre-menstrual symptoms.
- Women who take the pill are less likely to have certain gynaecological problems.

What are the disadvantages of the pill?

- If a woman is never going to have children, she will have to take the pill throughout her reproductive years. As she ages her risk of serious side effects increases.
- Women with certain medical conditions are unable to take the pill. A woman who smokes and takes the pill substantially increases her risk of serious side effects.
- Training the woman to take the pill regularly can be difficult.
- The woman may become pregnant if she forgets to take the pill and is sexually active.
- There may be side effects such as increasing weight, headaches, spotting between periods, and depression.
- Other medications, such as various anti-epileptic preparations, antibiotics and anti-depressants may interfere with the effectiveness of the pill or vice versa.

In some cases, if one type of pill proves unsuitable for a woman, there may be another brand which is better. Her doctor will be able to help with this.

The IUD

The intra-uterine device (IUD) is a small plastic or plastic and copper object which is placed in the woman's uterus or womb by a doctor. The procedure is usually carried out in a clinic or doctor's surgery with a local anaesthetic but it can also be inserted in a hospital under a general anaesthetic if required. Nylon threads attached to one end of the IUD extend from the uterus into the vagina, so that the woman can make sure the IUD is in place.

If the woman has not been informed about what to expect during an IUD insertion, the procedure can be emotionally upsetting and painful. Cramps can occur after the insertion for a few minutes or hours, or even occasionally for a few weeks. Sometimes there is spotting between periods in the first three months, and periods may be heavier.

What are the advantages of an IUD?

- It is not dependent on following directions.
- It is not dependent on motivation.
- It is separate from the sex act.
- It only needs occasional checking.

What are the disavantages of an IUD?

- A woman must check the strings regularly or have them checked by someone else to make sure that the IUD is still in place. This should be done monthly.
- There is some risk of pelvic infection, which may be difficult to detect in a woman with intellectual disability.
- The insertion and regular checkups can be upsetting for a woman who is fearful of internal examinations.
- The insertion may be painful and there may be bleeding afterwards.
- If menstrual management is a problem, this could be exacerbated by heavier bleeding after the IUD is inserted.

Depo-Provera

Depo-Provera is the most commonly used injectable contraceptive. It is an injection of the hormone progestagen, usually 150 mg, once every three months.

When it was first introduced, it seemed like the perfect form of contraception for women who had difficulties with other methods. Some doctors began prescribing it rather indiscriminately, without fully informing women of possible side effects. Consequently, there has been controversy about its use as a contraceptive in the United States, Australia and the United Kingdom. However, it is widely used in many countries, and there is no medical evidence that it increases cancer, which was one of the early concerns. It is available in Australia and the United Kingdom and can be used quite legally provided the woman or her substitute decision-maker is informed about possible side effects and gives an informed consent. It is not available in the United States for use as a contraceptive.

What are the advantages of Depo-Provera?

- Periods usually stop altogether after a few months (some people may consider this to be a disadvantage). Even where this does not happen the menstrual flow is usually reduced.

- It is extremely reliable.
- It is independent of the sex act.
- No instructions need to be followed.
- It is not dependent on motivation.
- There is no evidence that smoking increases possible side effects.

What are the disadvantages of Depo-Provera?

- There may be irregular spotting.
- A doctor must be seen every three months.
- The woman may not like the injections.
- Fertility may not return for up to two years after the last injection.
- There may be side effects such as weight gain and headaches, similar to those of the pill.
- It is not possible to reverse the effects. If a woman experiences side effects after the injection, these will last for three months or longer.

Whatever method of contraception is chosen, it is important for everyone involved to understand that regular medical checkups will need to be a part of the contraceptive routine. These checkups will include pap tests, pelvic examinations and breast checks. Residential care staff and parents should incorporate these into the woman's way of life.

Other Hormonal Methods

Some additional hormonal methods of contraception, such as Norplant which is inserted under the skin and vaginal rings which release low levels of hormone, are now available in the United States. However, in Australia and the United Kingdom these are still in the clinical trial stage and so they are not yet readily available. Potential side effects are likely to be similar to other hormonal preparations. Advantages will be similar to those of Depo-Provera.

Sterilisation

NARELLE: I went to the doctor about contraception but I can't take the pill, because of nerves, and he said I should get my tubes tied but I hate anything to do with hospitals and operations. So we talked it over and David thought he might have a vasectomy. He talked to the workshop manager, who thought it was a good idea, and then he talked to the doctor.

DAVID: But I was scared really, for a long time. But there were a lot of people who were very understanding, see, and didn't push me and let me take my time making up my mind. Then it was arranged that I go to the Family Planning clinic in Sydney. I didn't want to have it done in [country town] because they wanted to put me in hospital to do it and I'm scared of that. But at the Family Planning clinic, they explained everything and didn't rush me and it was terrific because they let Narelle come into the room while they were doing it.

NARELLE: I thought I would faint when I saw the blood but I didn't — I was so surprised.

DAVID: It's kind of brought us together, since then.

Sterilisation is a surgical procedure which permanently prevents a woman from conceiving a child or a man from fathering one. Sterilisation for women for purely contraceptive reasons is usually called tubal ligation. Sterilisation for men is called a vasectomy.

Vasectomy

Vasectomy is a simple, low risk procedure which is usually performed in a Family Planning clinic or doctor's surgery with a local anaesthetic. It can also be done in a hospital under a general anaesthetic if required.

It takes about fifteen minutes for the doctor to cut and seal the two tubes (vas deferens) which carry the sperm from the testes to the penis. After a vasectomy sperm and semen are still produced and semen still comes out of the man's penis when he ejaculates, but there are no sperm in the semen because they cannot get past the sealed point. Vasectomy does not affect sex, sex drive or hormone production. However, it does take about ten ejaculations after the vasectomy before the man can be sure that all the sperm have been cleared out of his tubes.

Tubal Ligation

Tubal ligation (or tubal sterilisation) is performed by cutting, 'burning', clipping or tying a section of each Fallopian tube. It is performed in a hospital under a general anaesthetic. One or two tiny incisions need to be made in the abdomen but the scarring is minimal and often under the bikini line. The woman is usually in hospital for a day, and may need a few days off work after that.

Tubal ligation is virtually 100 per cent reliable. The woman will still have her periods, still ovulate and produce hormones, and sex will be just the same.

Attempted reversals of tubal ligations are rarely successful and so it is considered to be a permanent method of contraception.

Hysterectomy

Hysterectomy is the removal of the uterus, and sometimes the ovaries as well. It is a major surgical procedure requiring a stay of at least a week in hospital, followed by a recovery period of eight weeks or more.

After a hysterectomy a woman does not menstruate, but she will continue to ovulate unless her ovaries are removed. Pre-menstrual symptoms will usually continue unless the ovaries are removed.

Hysterectomy should never be carried out as a method of contraception. It should only be done for a medical reason. Medical reasons might include excessive bleeding not responsive to other treatments, chronic pelvic inflammatory disease, cancer, fibroids or prolapse.

Some parents and carers request hysterectomy because it stops menstruation. And, certainly, menstrual management can be very difficult. However, in our experience most women, including some women with severe intellectual disability, can learn to manage their own menstruation providing they are taught in an appropriate way. Your Family Planning Association, Planned Parenthood Federation or a psychologist with experience in task analysis may be able to assist.

Endometrial Ablation

Endometrial ablation is a relatively new procedure. An electric current is passed through the lining of the uterus so that it changes. An endometrial ablation is usually carried out when a woman experiences painful, heavy periods which do not respond to other treatment. However, some people are now also recommending it for women with intellectual disability because it usually results in infertility and stops menstruation.

The procedure is done in a hospital under a general anaesthetic.

The woman will usually be in hospital for one day with a recovery period of about two weeks.

Issues Involved in Sterilisation

Parents, carers and people with intellectual disability need the opportunity to explore fully the many issues involved in sterilisation and hysterectomy. Sterilisation is sometimes seen as an easy solution to problems which it in fact cannot prevent or solve — problems like sexual assault and inappropriate behaviour.

Women with intellectual disability who are sterilised or given a hysterectomy without their knowledge or consent are often angry and resentful when they find out or realise why they don't have periods like their friends.

Legally, it is becoming more and more difficult for parents to have their child with intellectual disability sterilised. In many states parents are not able to consent to this procedure on behalf of their child, regardless of whether their child is an adult or a minor — consent can only be given legally by the person with intellectual disability (if he or she can give an informed decision) or by a Court or legally constituted tribunal, such as a Guardianship Board.

The more opportunities people with intellectual disability are given to develop social and decision-making skills, the more likely they are to develop the maturity and knowledge they need to make these decisions for themselves. Besides, removing a body organ or rendering someone infertile is a major invasion of personal rights.

For people with intellectual disability to give informed consent, they must understand not only that the procedure involves an operation, but also that it means they will never be able to have children.

Summary

To help you decide whether a person with intellectual disability should be considering contraception or sterilisation, you may like to consider the following questions.

- Is the person sexually active or likely to become sexually active in the near future?
- What is the likelihood of the person being sexually assaulted?
- Can the person or his or her partner assume personal responsibility for using a contraceptive?
- How much does the person understand or want to understand about contraception?

- Is the person motivated to use contraception?
- Does the person want to be a parent now or in the future? Does the person understand the responsibilities of parenting?
- What are the person's past experiences in receiving medical care? Does he or she have any particular fears in this regard? For a woman, has she ever had a gynaecological examination?
- How does the person feel about his or her body? (for example, in relation to condom use)
- Can the person give his or her own medical history, or will a carer or parent need to be present at the doctor's?
- What resources are available for teaching the person how to use or manage the chosen method of contraception?
- Are there other people who need to be involved in the decision? (for example a partner, parents, carers)

Abortion

Unfortunately, unplanned and unwanted pregnancies do occur, often causing a great deal of distress and anxiety for those involved. In this situation, the options are abortion, adoption or fostering, or keeping the child.

An early abortion, that is up to about twelve weeks of pregnancy, is a relatively simple medical procedure and can be done with a local anaesthetic in a clinic or doctor's surgery. The contents of the uterus are removed through the vagina, usually by suction. However, if the pregnancy is further advanced the woman will have to go into labour and deliver the foetus that way, which can be quite painful and emotionally distressing. This is usually done in hospital.

Sometimes the decision of whether to abort or not is made more difficult by the fact that the pregnancy is not detected until it is well advanced. Carers or parents may not be aware that the woman is sexually active or that contraception is not being used successfully. In an advanced pregnancy abortion is much riskier and often more traumatic.

Sometimes the decision is made difficult by the fact that if there was sufficient time to educate the woman about her options she would be able to make an informed decision herself, but such time is not available. Planned Parenthood or Family Planning may be able to provide counselling in this situation.

Abortion may also be a problematic option if you live in a state where abortion is illegal. Abortion laws vary widely from state to state. It is vital to find out from a reliable source the legal status of abortion in your state. Family Planning Associations or Planned Parenthood Federations will be able to provide you with this information. The person legally allowed to give consent to the procedure where the woman cannot give informed consent herself, also varies from state to state.

In practice, parents and workers have a strong responsibility to ensure that people with intellectual disability are given adequate sex education and access to contraception so that the chances of an unplanned, unwanted pregnancy are diminished.

Chapter 16
SEXUAL ASSAULT

An eighteen-year-old man had recently obtained a part-time job in the laundry of a large hospital. He had to walk through a large park and an area of bush on his way to and from work. His parents, although very pleased that he had got the job, were terrified that he would be sexually assaulted. He had had no sex education.

One of the major fears of parents with a child who has intellectual disability is that their child will be sexually assaulted. This is common to parents regardless of whether the child is male or female, although parents with a daughter have the additional concern that their daughter may become pregnant.

Unfortunately, research indicates that this fear is realistic — a far higher proportion of people with intellectual disability are sexually assaulted than non-disabled people. And, although it is often difficult for parents to accept, the research also indicates that the person with intellectual disability is far more likely to be sexually assaulted by someone they know, for example a family member, friend or carer, than a stranger.

Sexual assault was previously called rape. It includes not just sexual intercourse without consent, but also unwanted sexual touching, forcing a person to touch another in sexual ways, and forcing a person to see or hear something sexual. Even threatening any of these is a criminal offence. And some states have particularly stiff penalties for carers who betray a position of trust by sexually assaulting their clients.

People with intellectual disability can be particularly vulnerable to sexual assault because they are less likely to resist, less likely to report, and if they do report less likely to be believed. Even if they are believed action is less likely to be taken because of the perceived difficulties associated with their credibility in court.

⎰ Sexual assault is first and foremost an act of violence. Many victims of sexual assault feel guilty after the event, although the effects of sexual assault on a person are as varied as the person experiencing them. It is important to remember that no behaviour, however foolish or provocative it appears, is ever a justification for sexual assault.

The following strategies are important if a person reveals to you that he or she has been sexually assaulted. Listen to them carefully and acknowledge that you have understood what they have said and accept it. Tell them that they have done the right thing by telling you, that it is not their fault, and that you will try to have it stopped. Tell them about the options that they have, including short and long-term medical and counselling services. Promise as much confidentiality as you can. Make accurate notes, as these may be needed later. Do not confront the alleged perpetrator — the authorities will do this. And if legal action is taken make sure that the person with disability has a support person (this could be a worker from a Sexual Assault centre) and that he or she understands the police and court procedures.

Avoid letting different people question the person with intellectual disability over and over again, as this may make the victim feel that it is he or she who is guilty.

If the person has been assaulted very recently, and he or she is agreeable, arrange medical treatment and counselling as soon as possible, for example at a Sexual Assault or Rape Crisis centre. A physical examination will be done, along with tests for pregnancy and sexually transmitted diseases. Counselling services are also available for people who have been sexually assaulted in the past but have only disclosed it recently.

Parents or staff may also find this a difficult and distressing time. It is important that they too receive support, especially if they are assisting the person with disability in laying charges.

Parents and carers can greatly help people with intellectual disability resist sexual assault by ensuring that they have well developed self-esteem and assertiveness skills. In addition, the sex education of people with disability should make it possible for them to identify when any person (not only a stranger) is approaching them in an inappropriate or unacceptable way. And they also need to know what to do and who to tell when this happens.

One very effective method of teaching people with intellectual disability how to identify inappropriate behaviour is the Circles Concept. Your local school or intellectual disability service may be able to tell you how to teach these concepts in a way that makes them easy for the person with intellectual disability to understand. The Circles Concept has been successfully taught to some people with severe intellectual disability. See pages 21–23 for more information on the Circles Concept.

Incest

Incest is sexual assault by a family member. There are specialist services in this area which provide counselling for victims. Some states also have rehabilitation services for perpetrators.

The Sex Offender with Intellectual Disability

People with intellectual disability are often accused of sexually harassing or assaulting others. There is even a mythology that men with intellectual disability have a high sexual libido and poor impulse control. Sometimes they are accused because they look different or because their behaviour is inappropriate — they may masturbate or expose themselves in public or urinate in a strange way. Sometimes excessive displays of affection are misinterpreted as being sexual. However, despite all of the above, some people with intellectual disability do commit sexual assault.

In many cases inappropriate behaviours and sometimes even sexual assaults result from insufficient or inappropriate education. Poor modelling, for example, in institutions or even in the home, can teach the person with intellectual disability that these behaviours are acceptable. That is why it is vital to teach the child with intellectual disability appropriate social and sexual behaviours from the beginning. They need to know about public and private parts of the body, and that private parts of the body should only be exposed in private places. They need to know that private behaviours usually involve private parts of the body and that these are also only for private places. They need to know that just as their body belongs only to them, and should not be touched by others unless they give permission, likewise other people's bodies belong to them, and should not be touched unless permission is given.

Of course, there is a very small number of men with intellectual disability who offend not through lack of appropriate sex education, but for the same reasons as non-disabled offenders. In these cases the offenders will require a different approach, such as a trained therapist, as their behaviour will rarely respond to education alone.

Sexual Harassment

Sexual harassment is unwelcome and uninvited sexual conduct by a person who stands or is perceived to stand in a position of power over the person with intellectual disability, for example, it could be a person providing a service.

Sexual harassment includes behaviour such as kissing, touching and pinching, sexual propositions, attempts at sexual intercourse, offensive gestures, repeated sexual jokes or innuendos and persistent staring or leering.

Sexual harassment is against the law in many states. Again, the person with intellectual disability needs to learn that he or she has the right to say no and the right not to be subjected to this sort of behaviour. It is also important to know where to get help if it is required.

Chapter 17
SEXUALITY AND AGING

As people with intellectual disability age, they may confront many changes in their lives in addition to body changes.

For those who have lived with their parents all their lives, it may happen that they will have to confront their parents' deaths and changes in their accommodation at the same time. Or the change in accommodation may occur because parents become unable to continue to provide care and support for their son or daughter with intellectual disability.

These changes are significant and it is to be expected that people with intellectual disability will, like others, experience feelings of grief, anger and confusion. Withdrawal or challenging behaviours may accompany these feelings and adjustment may be very difficult.

For those who have spent a lifetime working, retirement will present a new lifestyle which will also require a certain amount of adjustment.

In addition, since older people in our society are not expected to be sexual, older people with intellectual disability may find their needs for intimacy and their sexual heath needs doubly ignored.

The impact of the aging process and the events which accompany it need to be acknowledged by those around the person with intellectual disability, and appropriate support provided. This support could include education about body and lifestyle changes, counselling to deal with bereavement, or placing the person in contact with services for the aged.

Women

Most women experience menopause or the 'change of life' between the ages of forty-five and fifty, although some experience it earlier and some later. At this time the levels of the female hormone oestrogen reduce and certain body changes occur as a consequence.

The most obvious sign is that menstruation stops. Other symptoms can include hot flushes, headaches, extreme tiredness and mood swings. Most women go through menopause with little or no discomfort. However, a sizeable minority experience extreme discomfort and require treatment.

The drop in oestrogen causes a reduction in vaginal lubrication which can make intercourse painful. The possibility of vaginal infection and cystitis is also increased. Any vaginal problems should be investigated by a doctor to identify the cause and prescribe appropriate treatment.

The drop in oestrogen in conjunction with other factors can also contribute to osteoporosis or weakness of the bones which makes them more susceptible to breaks.

Hormone Replacement Therapy or HRT can be used by doctors to relieve the symptoms of menopause when they are distressing and also to treat osteoporosis. However, some women with certain medical conditions cannot have this type of treatment, and there are also risks associated with its use. Women and their carers need to be made fully aware of these issues and any alternatives by the doctor, before a decision is made to use Hormone Replacement Therapy. Women who are using HRT should also be aware that their periods may start again.

Women who are sexually active with men will still need to use contraception for at least a year after menstruation has stopped to ensure that they do not become pregnant. Note that age makes some forms of contraception less desirable and the options should be discussed with a doctor.

Women who have been using Depo-Provera on a long-term basis for menstrual management or contraception will no longer require its prescription after menopause. However, the use of Depo-Provera may make the time of menopause difficult to determine. Doctors usually cease the use of Depo-Provera when the woman is between forty-five and fifty years of age.

In summary, women's sexual health continues to be of significance until death. Pap tests, breast checks and sexual health monitoring need to be continued on a regular basis. Women should be educated to understand the changes in their body that accompany aging, and encouraged to maintain good health with appropriate exercise and diet. Carers should be alert to the symptoms described in this section so that they can arrange treatment for women who may not be able to seek it out for themselves.

Men

Both men and women may notice a slower sexual arousal time as they age. Men may have more difficulty in getting and maintaining an erection, and ejaculation may be less noticeable. Explaining to men that these changes are a normal part of aging may alleviate concern about them.

Sperm production generally ceases in the mid-seventies, although it can last longer. It is safer to assume a man is fertile unless it is known otherwise.

Many men over fifty experience problems with their prostate gland. The prostate gland forms part of the male reproductive system and is located beneath the bladder. Pain is the most obvious symptom, although sometimes a white discharge may also be noticed. Diagnosis should be made by a doctor. Most problems respond to non-surgical treatment.

As with women, general sexual health should continue to be monitored.

There are many medical problems that can occur as people age which may have an effect on their sexual interest or sexual functioning. The sexual aspect should be considered when treating these medical problems and when prescribing medication as some medications can also have an effect.

It is generally agreed that continuing sexual activity, including masturbation, into old age helps keep those body parts functioning well and has positive psychological effects. Middle and old age are phases of one's whole life. As they age, people with intellectual disability, like other people, should be assisted to lead a life which is as full and as healthy as possible.

Chapter 18
PARENTAL CONCERNS ABOUT GROUP HOMES

A growing number of parents now believe that their son or daughter with intellectual disability does have the right to express his or her sexuality in an appropriate way. However, this belief raises problems about who will provide appropriate sex education if the person is living in a community home.

In cases where the person with intellectual disability now lives in a group home, parents may question the competence of residential staff to implement programs of sex education. In Australia a large proportion of residential staff is very young and without professional training. Many such staff are students and have a very responsible and thoughtful approach to their role. However, others are 'passing through' and have not yet made up their minds as to their future career. As a result, and because of the stress of the job, staff turnover is very high. In one community house for instance, there are four permanent staff, but throughout the year more than thirty-five casual staff are used.

This situation gives rise to a rather unsettled environment and causes much concern for parents. It is very difficult to implement consistent education programs under these conditions and particularly hard to ensure consistency in attitude and orientation in the area of sexuality.

However, parents should not despair. Undergraduate level courses in residential care are now being offered in Australia and in many parts of the United States. Government services in Australia offer fairly comprehensive staff training programs, as do some privately run charitable associations. It is also becoming more common, and in some cases mandatory, to involve parents in the management of residential services. Where possible parents should become involved in decisions concerning management to ensure that sex education programs are appropriate and relevant. It is vital to promote the view that parents are partners in the endeavour to establish fulfilling lives for their sons and daughters.

82

In any society, there will be cultural and social differences, particularly in regard to what is or is not acceptable to include in a sex education program, or what should be the limits of sexual expression. Family mores and belief systems can also be very strong.

If people with intellectual disability who need support to make decisions about their lives, are to be respected, then they must be accorded the right to have their social, cultural and familial background acknowledged and represented through the involvement of their families.

Sexual Issues in a Respite Care Home

A large proportion of adults with intellectual disability live at home with their families. Some are lucky to have the opportunity to spend some of their time in a respite care house. In one such house a number of issues relating to sexuality had arisen and the respite care staff requested policy guidelines from the Parent Advisory Committee.

The issues were as follows:

1. One regular respite care client frequently hired soft pornographic videos to watch when he stayed overnight. He would watch them on the VCR in the communal living room. He was used to watching them with his father at home. Staff were concerned because one or two of the residents were much younger and appeared to become quite agitated when these videos were on. Other residents complained because they wanted to choose other videos.

2. A client, while staying in the respite house, invited a friend to dinner and then had the friend to stay overnight in her bedroom, sharing the bed. One parent of another client objected strongly.

The Parent Advisory Committee, which consisted of parent representatives, was divided on these issues, as were the staff. So they decided that the clients should have the final say in the decisions.

Before eliciting opinions from the clients it was necessary to first determine each person's understanding of the issues. A psychological consultant, experienced in sexuality programming, and three staff members, designed and administered a questionnaire to all the people who stayed at the respite house during one selected month. The questionnaire consisted of pictures relating to sexual knowledge.

Nineteen people received the questionnaire. Of these seven demonstrated sufficient understanding of sexuality to be asked the questions relating to the issues which had arisen in the respite home.

On the basis of these responses the following guidelines were drawn up and accepted by the Parent Advisory Committee.

Guidelines for Staff in Dealing with Specific Situations which May Arise in Adult Respite Care

Erotic movies

Some clients are in the habit of borrowing erotic movies and watching them at home. This is permissible in respite care with the following restrictions:

1. The following types of movies are not acceptable
   - Those involving violence or deviant sexuality e.g. sadism.
   - Those which specifically exploit/degrade women.
2. Discussion should occur before leaving for the video hire shop on types of movies to be chosen.
3. Only those clients who are interested should have to watch these movies. A time and place to watch them should be negotiated, and alternative activities arranged for clients who do not wish to watch them.

A client wanting a non-client friend (of either sex) to stay overnight at the respite care house

1. 'Friends' are allowed to stay occasionally (e.g. if it's not possible for them to go home late at night) but they should sleep on the sofa.
2. Clients should not have friends to stay overnight with them, in their bed, while they are staying in adult respite care.

If two clients are found engaging in sexual activity together while in respite care

Generally speaking, sexual activity between clients while in respite care is not acceptable, because it is not their home and because the risks of infection, pregnancy and exploitation are too great.

However, if they are accidentally discovered in one of the bedrooms, that is, in a private place, the following guidelines apply:

1. If one party appears to be unwilling, the staff member should interrupt the act and counsel both about not having sex with someone who does not want to.

   Also, because this situation constitutes sexual assault, sexual assault guidelines should be put into action. The person who has been assaulted should be supported and counselled at the time. As soon as possible, the house staff should contact the Community Team Leader, who will in turn contact the nearest Sexual Assault Service. The Community Team Leader should ensure that the client's family is informed, and in conjunction with the staff at the Sexual Assault Service should advise the client about his or her right to report the matter to the police.

2. If both parties appear to be willing, the staff member should leave them in privacy but counsel them later concerning house rules.
3. If the couple are in a public part of the house, they should be interrupted in a quiet, dignified manner.
4. If both parties appear to be willing, the staff do not have a responsibility to inform the families of the incident, unless the situation is considered detrimental to one party. Clients may, however, be asked if they wish to inform their families. The client's decision in this matter is to be respected.

If there is disagreement between staff and families concerning the client's rights to sexual expression

The staff should provide factual information to parents about the rights of clients. If no agreement can be reached, the staff should suggest further discussions at which the family's caseworker and the client should be present.

What can we learn from this example?

- A wide variety of issues can arise when people have to live together in close proximity.
- People in the same community can have very different attitudes to sexuality.
- People using a particular respite house can have different levels of understanding, resulting in different levels of participation in decision making.
- A person's sexuality is an intensely personal and private matter, and decisions concerning it require great respect and tact.

It is vital that staff and parents find time to explore these issues together in an atmosphere of mutual respect and trust. Both staff and parents may need to adopt more flexible attitudes as well as learn new facts. The job of assisting adults to make very personal decisions about their lives is extremely unusual and demanding, and should not be undertaken lightly.

Note that any decision made in response to a situation like the ones outlined above, will depend to some extent on the particular set of circumstances and the individuals involved.

Chapter 19

DEVELOPING A SEXUALITY POLICY FOR YOUR ORGANISATION

In the previous chapter we discussed a real life situation which led to the development of a policy on sexuality in a respite care house.

The advantage of having a policy on sexuality in an organisation is that people then know where they stand — parents are aware of what practices are permitted in the home, staff are aware of their professional obligations and clients know their rights and responsibilities.

There will be some limits on the development of the policy. For example, it must be consistent with state or country laws. This means that if a law upholds the right of adults to choose and be involved with a sexual partner, then an organisational policy cannot prohibit them from doing so. Similarly, if legislation prohibits people with intellectual disability from marrying an organisation cannot act against this, although it can lobby for legislative change.

Developing a policy can be a time-consuming and difficult process. It can result in some very emotional debates among parents, staff and clients. However, it can also be an educative process which enhances co-operation and relationships.

Policy development which involves all those with an interest is much more likely to be implemented than policy which is developed and imposed by one person such as a Chief Executive Officer. People with an interest include clients, parents, staff, management, funding bodies and any potential opposition or organisations which will support the policy.

The process of developing the policy may be speeded up by getting a small working party or sub-committee to write a draft discussion paper, distribute it and then invite comment. The draft discussion paper could be based on policies from other organisations, which have been modified to suit the needs of the organisation in question. This saves reinventing the wheel completely. The draft discussion paper should also include a rationale for having a policy.

Before the consultation process begins and the policy is written, a time frame should be established and the parameters or limits of the policy decided. It is also necessary to decide on an endorsement procedure.

To ensure that the policy is implemented once it is endorsed, all staff, clients and other relevant people need to be informed of its contents and educated about how it will work in practice.

A Sample Draft Policy

Principles

1. People with intellectual disability have the same rights as other people in the community to form and maintain relationships, including sexual relationships.

2. People with intellectual disability have the right to education about human relationships and sexuality. This education should be presented in such a way as to maximise the individual's ability to learn. As well as information, it should cover the areas of values and skills development. It should be age appropriate and culturally sensitive.

3. People with intellectual disability have the right to be free of exploitation, including sexual exploitation and harassment.

4. Staff are responsible for assisting clients to develop a positive self-image. They can do this by encouraging personal development and the acquisition of appropriate social skills.

5. Staff working with people with intellectual disability must have access to education in human relations and sexuality in order to effectively implement policy.

6. People with intellectual disability have the right to preventive and curative health measures in sexual and reproductive health.

7. Each individual has the right to choose his or her own values.

8. People with intellectual disability have the legal right to marry and to have children. They should have access to education and counselling on conception, contraception and parenting, and to genetic counselling, to enable them to make informed decisions on these issues.

9. Where a person with intellectual disability is unable to make an informed decision, the appropriate legally designated authority

[name this person or people] will be responsible for making the decision.

10. Where there are difficulties with menstrual management, all methods of training must be properly trialled before hormonal or surgical intervention is considered.

11. Where the person with intellectual disability is a child, the family and staff should work together as partners in developing age-appropriate relationship and sex education programs.

12. Where a child is concerned, the family should in most cases be the primary source of sexual values and knowledge.

Policies

1. Staff working in this service will uphold the principles outlined in this document, and follow the associated guidelines.

2. Staff will assist clients with intellectual disability to assert their rights, practise their responsibilities and avoid exploitation in the area of sexuality, by providing or ensuring access to appropriate sex education.

3. Staff will at all times assist people with intellectual disability to develop social skills and patterns of behaviour which will enhance the development of close personal relationships, including sexual relationships and marriage.

4. Staff will act to prevent sexual exploitation of persons with disability.

5. Medication or surgery for contraception or menstrual management will be considered on an individual basis, taking into account the person's medical history, age and lifestyle. If possible the client must give informed consent; otherwise the appropriate legally designated authority [name this person or people] is responsible for making the decision.

6. Staff will have education, such as inservice courses, in human relations and sexuality.

Chapter 20
SEX EDUCATION IN A WORKSHOP SETTING

〈 Although we have talked primarily about parents and workers as sex educators, it is obvious that sex education does not stop there.〉 When people with intellectual disability reach adulthood, they often move from school to employment, sometimes in a sheltered workshop, or increasingly to supported or open employment. Here, new opportunities for social interaction arise, and with them the need for help in coping in a new environment.

'The workshop was like a new world to me. I was pretty confused at first. It took me a long time to understand how things worked. I could not make friends for a long time. I was too shy and frightened.'

The Sexuality Group
'Please miss, why was I born retarded?'

The canteen tables in the sheltered workshop had been cleared. A small group of workers were staying to listen to the 'sex lady'. Everyone clustered eagerly around the laminex tables.

'We are all born different,' the educator began. 'Some of us are born with disability, some of us are born geniuses. Some of us have red hair and some brown. Some need to wear glasses and some can't walk and need wheelchairs. But we have all been born into this world, we are all different and we are all special.' Some nodded their heads. Others sat up straighter.

'But let me ask you a question? What does being born mean?' the educator continued.

'It's babies, a baby gets borned.'

'The belly-button.'

'You come out of Mummy's tummy.'

'You get a tummy-ache.'

'You gotta get married to have babies.'

'You gotta put your . . . put your. . . .' Giggles from the others. Some glanced at the educator, waiting for her reaction.

'Penis,' she supplied calmly. Some of her audience gasped.

'Yeah, you gotta put your penis in the 'gina,' continued the young man. There were screams of laughter. Some glared at him.

'Don't be rude, Peter,' one said sternly.

The age range in this workshop was sixteen to thirty-six years. Surely there is a problem with our education system and our social conditioning if adults of this age go into the workforce with such an inadequate understanding of relationships, responsibility, social behaviour and sex.

The educator pointed to a couple of large cloth doll models, a male and a female, and began a discussion about the physical differences between men and women. Everyone loved the models which were a far cry from the beautiful people constantly depicted on the TV and in magazines. They laughed and at times felt embarrassed, but were still able to learn the right words for the different body parts, and understand the importance of hygiene, privacy and not letting people touch you when they shouldn't.

As everyone relaxed, the questions came thick and fast. 'Why do people have sex? What do people do in sex? What is masturbation? Can it make you sick? What are periods? How young can you become pregnant? What's a prostitute? Do a boy and girl have to get married to have sex? How do you get VD? What is AIDS? What is oral sex?'

A sheltered home, work and school life can lead to misinformation, confusion and anxiety.

Why answer these questions at all? Because not answering them puts people in a very vulnerable position. We know that in relative terms there is far more exploitation of people with intellectual disability than of non-disabled people. The protective environment in which many people with intellectual disability grow up paradoxically results in their becoming psychologically and physically endangered. Also, withholding such information implies a lack of respect and a denial of the sexuality of such people. It can never be too strongly emphasised that most people with intellectual disability undergo the same sexual development and have the same sexual needs as other adults of their age.

A Staff Member's View

'When we first started sex education at the workshop, only two parents objected to their children being included. The most wonderful thing that happened was the tremendous effect on the workers of seeing a film about birth. It was like a revelation to them. No one had ever spoken to them about how babies are born, let alone shown them a film.

'The way we got started on this was that we noticed many people in the workshop were either having difficulties in their relationshops or were expressing themselves sexually in very inappropriate ways or in inappropriate places, for instance, by masturbating at the work bench or trying to have intercourse in the canteen. Because they had been treated as children for so long, they didn't know how to act. It isn't that it was happening a lot, but it only takes one incident like that to upset staff and others. So we called in a sex educator first of all to talk to us, the staff, and to help us to work out a sex education program, and also to help us just to come to terms with the whole issue of sex. We also agreed that it was better for staff to handle the program, rather than an educator from outside, because staff are on the spot to deal with questions which might arise after the program. Some staff members didn't want to take part in the program and that was alright; only those who were willing to undertake the program themselves were included in it.

'I always treat them as equals and they always respond as equals. With a sex education program they learn to trust you. They learn that they can talk about things that worry them and how to ask for advice. Because whether parents and other people like it or not, sex and relationshops occupy a large part of our people's minds, just as they do with all young people.

'But the thing I learnt most from the sex education program was how to deal with sex-related problems when they arose in the workshop. The program gave me and other staff members a chance to think through the issues and work out in advance how we really felt about things like masturbation, contraception, couples living together, homosexuality, abortion, sterilisation. Sooner or later one or another, or all of these issues will come up and we won't have to panic because, having already thought these things through, we can work out solutions without getting emotional.

'For instance, we had a couple who were having sexual intercourse in the park opposite the railway station. We were able to talk to them reasonably, explain to them that their behaviour was inappropriate and work out alternatives with them. We brought the parents in as well and talked to them. Although at first they were shocked, we were able to explain to them that their children were adults and that they were behaving this way because they did not have anywhere else to go.

'We always advise parents to give their adult children, in as natural a way as possible, opportunities for privacy so they can be together with their partners without hassles. For instance, we suggest the parents occasionally go out for the evening and leave the couple by themselves for a few hours. In most cases parents can see the point of that and co-operate. Then we have fewer problems at the workshop as well.

'There is another couple who live together. We are fairly sure that they are not having a sexual relationship, but they get on well with each other and the arrangement works well. Everyone needs companionship.

'The point is that everyone needs someone else, and people will seek out ways of getting together, whether it's for simple friendship or whether there is a sexual side to their needs as well. There is no way of protecting people from that. Protection is not keeping people segregated, protection is teaching people how to behave towards each other and to themselves. Like using contraception, like finding a private place to be together so they don't offend other people, and how not to force someone to have sex with you if they don't want it, but to use the outlet of masturbation in an appropriate way in private.

'There are other issues that have to be dealt with as well. For instance, some of the men at the workshop go to prostitutes and get terribly exploited. Other men go to prostitutes, but they don't get exploited because they know how to deal with them.

'Our people don't know how to deal with this sort of thing unless someone teaches them about exploitation in this specific situation. People with intellectual disability have great difficulty in generalising from one situation to another. They have problems with such concepts as "exploitation". They have to be taught how to act in each situation. You can't help them by pretending that these situations don't happen.

'Another man we know who works in one of the other workshops goes into public toilets and looks for homosexual encounters. Now, that could be dangerous for him in many ways, but you can't deal with the problem if you pretend that such a thing doesn't happen or if you try to stop him without suggesting realistic alternatives which are appropriate for him.

'There was an incident a while ago in one workshop where a twenty-four-year-old girl was found having intercourse with a man on the workshop floor. She came from a wealthy family who had protected her very closely. Recently, they had gone overseas and had left her in a convent to be looked after by the nuns. The stunned supervisor couldn't believe that she was capable of having sex or that she knew anything about it. The girl assured the supervisor that she knew all about it because the milkman at the convent had "taught" her. She didn't know there was anything wrong in what she was doing and she certainly had no understanding of the implications of the act. So that kind of "protection" can be positively dangerous.

'Now that we have regular sex education programs, more of our people are coming to us seeking sterilisation, because they have made up their own minds that they do not want children. We have a very understanding doctor nearby who knows our people and how to talk with them about birth control and about sterilisation. He also does all the regular medical checkups for all the women here. I feel this is an important part of our program because we can follow through and give people support in all these matters. I think the sheltered workshop has a big part to play in the development of the person with intellectual disability. For many people work is the first step towards independence and for many people with intellectual disability who live at home, the workshop is their only social outlet away from the home. Most of them are totally unprepared to deal with the new situation. They badly need social training, as well as training in appropriate sexual behaviour. Even if their parents and the school were giving them proper training in these areas, they would still need this kind of education in the work environment, because it is a new social context.

'There should be ongoing programs in all settings. The staff need to be trained to deal with the topic of sexuality. Sometimes some of the workers just go wild with the freedom and start having relationships all over the place, and some of them get hurt too. Yes, there can be a lot of emotional ups and downs then. Sometimes you can see they have just been allowed to go up to anyone and start touching and cuddling up — that may be alright at home, but it can lead to serious trouble outside.

'You have to be pretty firm with them sometimes, and some of them never learn. We have one woman at the workshop — she's in her forties, and didn't come to the workshop until she was thirty-six years old. She had been living at home in a very protective environment. She goes up to men in the street and tries to touch them and take their hand. We are trying to do something about it but it's hard because she's been doing it for so long.'

Chapter 21
RUNNING A FORMAL SEX EDUCATION PROGRAM

Many people with learning difficulties find it more difficult than others to articulate their questions and concerns about sexuality. It is hard for them to understand the constant barrage of often inaccurate and misleading messages on television and in films and popular magazines. It is often difficult for them to get clear, simple and correct information from those around them or from books and magazines. However, this does not mean that their sexuality is not important to them or that they don't have worries about it. It calls for a great deal of sensitivity and patience to get in touch with these unspoken needs and to provide information, skills and support.

We have talked a great deal in this book about informal methods of sex education, and of course these are vital. However, at various times in an individual's life, formal sex education programs are also important, to tie together in a coherent form the informal teaching, to provide a structure and to teach specific skills that are more easily learnt in a structured setting with other people.

This chapter explains some of the fundamentals for those interested in running a formal sex education program. Such people will be referred to as 'the educator' in this chapter, although it is not assumed that they have had any formal teacher training.

What are the Benefits of Sex Education?

⟨For people with intellectual disability, knowledge about their body and feelings can emphasise their similarities to others, despite their disability, and enable them to feel good about the things that make them an individual. For example, for some women with disabilities, the onset of their periods enables them, for the first time, to identify as a woman, and they experience the event very positively. ⟩

Sex education programs can assist people with intellectual disability to become aware of their needs and enable them to differentiate between friendship, love and sexual attraction. Such programs can assist personal decision-making about the type of relationship an individual wants, and teach them the words and behaviour necessary to communicate those decisions. Such strategies help prevent sexual exploitation and socially inappropriate behaviour — two of the greatest concerns for parents and staff. Sex education programs can also encourage responsible contraceptive use and realistic attitudes towards the responsibilities of parenting.

For people with intellectual disability, developing a sense of themselves and an ability to be assertive about their needs and desires will help to build self-esteem, which is an integral component of education about sexuality.

One question often asked by staff and parents, and by sex educators, is do people with intellectual disability actually learn anything in sex education programs. Research tells us that the answer to this question is yes. Sharynne Robinson did a study in Australia, in which she tested four groups of men and women both before and after sex education programs. In all cases, the level of understanding after the program increased and interviews with staff about the participants indicated that, in addition, people's general behaviour and social skills improved, and the level of socially inappropriate behaviour decreased. Winifred Kempton in the United States came to the same conclusions when she evaluated thirty-one courses which had showed her slides on Sexuality and the Mentally Handicapped to a total of 430 students with intellectual disability. She reported that staff were not aware of any serious inappropriate behaviour that could be attributed to the programs, and in fact reported an improvement in social behaviour, increased self-respect, more openness and fewer feelings of guilt. Books by these authors are included in the Resources section at the end of this book.

Of course, formal sex education can be done on an individual basis. However, there are often advantages in doing sex education in a group. These include the opportunity for participants to hear the viewpoints of other participants, and also the opportunity to improve peer relating skills. Some people with intellectual disability lack good peer relating skills because of the way they have been socialised to relate primarily to people in authority positions. Good peer relating skills are a vital part of improving relationship skills in general.

Most people with intellectual disability have similar aspirations to non-disabled people, that is, to be in an intimate relationship and to have a partner. Well-rounded sex education includes social and relationship skills which can enhance people's prospects in this area.

For most people with intellectual disability, the ability to reach a useful level of understanding about sexual issues and the accompanying skills is limited only by the lack of suitable programs.

Some myths that you may need to dispel before you can run your program are the following:

- *Providing sex education encourages people to have sex.*
  Research shows that this is not the case. In fact, not providing education may result in people experimenting in order to satisfy their curiosity.

- *Providing sex education encourages an interest in sex in people who would otherwise have had no such interest.*
  Information in various forms about sexuality permeates our society. Good sex education dispels myths, corrects misinformation and promotes socially appropriate behaviour.

- *Young people will be told too much too soon.*
  Children only absorb the amount and kind of information which satisfies their curiosity at that moment. They usually disregard the rest.

- *People with intellectual disability cannot learn, so it is a waste of time trying to teach them.*
  Different people are able to learn different things in different ways. Different people have different needs in learning. Research indicates that even people with severe intellectual disability are able to learn about appropriate social behaviour, body parts and, for women, menstrual management techniques.

Attitudes of the Sex Educator

Every person has values and attitudes regarding various aspects of sexuality, including sex educators. In the case of sex educators, however, it is essential that they are aware of their own values and attitudes, and how they obtained them. They also need to be aware of the ways in which they convey those values and attitudes to others. Sex educators have to accept that others have the right to have values and attitudes which differ from their own. While it is appropriate for an educator to encourage values and attitudes which, for example, will discourage sexual assault, it is not appropriate for them to advocate only certain sorts of relationships or sexual preferences. That is up to the individual, although the educator has a valuable role in providing information about options and encouraging group participants to consider consequences.

How Do I Acquire Teaching Skills?

Some of you will come to running formal sex education courses with a background in teaching and others will not. For those of you who do not, it is especially important for you to seek assistance to ensure that the sessions you run are based on sound educational practice, so that your teaching will be effective. There are lots of different ways to teach the same information and skills — these are called different teaching methods or strategies. Even those who do have a background in teaching may want some assistance if they have not taught people with intellectual disability before. They may also need to increase their knowledge of resources.

Family Planning Associations or Planned Parenthood Federations may have specialist educators with experience in teaching people with intellectual disability. They may also have useful information or resources which they hire out. They may even run teaching courses for disability workers who wish to implement sex education.

While you run your programs you may find it valuable to have an identified support person for yourself. This would be someone with whom you could discuss different teaching strategies, issues that arise in sessions and so on.

Creating a Good Learning Environment

Teaching adults is different from teaching children in that adults already have a lifetime of experiences behind them. This means that they come to any learning experience already armed with certain perceptions, information, values and attitudes and some skills.

In relation to sexuality the adult may have had positive experiences, such as a warm and supportive family when they were growing up and positive intimate relationships, or they may have had negative experiences, such as sexual abuse or exploitation, being labelled because of their disability, or being admonished for being sexual with someone else or masturbating. If people are experiencing a degree of fear, negativity, anxiety or embarrassment, then it is important to deal with this first, because such feelings can inhibit effective learning.

The values and attitudes that people hold can also limit their learning. If a person has been led to believe that anything sexual is dirty, wrong or bad, then he or she is not going to feel very comfortable in a sex education program. If this is the case, you may need to do some work on values and why people hold them and how different people hold different values before looking at information or skills development in your program. Sometimes a group participant may decide that the program is not for them.

You may find that many participants have misinformation. And depending on the source of that misinformation, you may have a lot of trouble convincing the person with intellectual disability that your information is the correct information, especially if their misinformation came from a significant person such as a parent or close friend, or the television.

There are several ways in which an educator can ensure a good learning environment. Make sure that the information presented is relevant to the learner. Deal with negative experiences and fears sensitively and carefully. Present the information in a way which is able to be understood by the learner, for example, do not use medical terminology when teaching body parts to people with intellectual disability — start with the terminology that they use themselves. Present information in an interesting and interactive way — if people are interested in the subject matter they will be more motivated to learn.

Setting Up Your Group

In setting up your group, consider the following points:

- The size of the group should depend on your group participants. When people have severe disabilities or behavioural problems a group of four may be optimum. When people have good social skills up to ten participants can work well.

- One of the advantages of teaching in groups is that participants can exchange experiences and views, and improve their social skills. For this reason, a mixed sex group is usually preferable. However, there may be cases, such as when a person has been sexually assaulted, where a mixed sex group would not be appropriate, or at least not initially. And there may be topics which are only relevant to one sex. For example, although it is important for both males and females to know about menstruation, training in menstrual management will only be of interest to women and girls.

- Groups with widely varying levels of ability, or in which a minority of participants have significant other disabilities such as visual or hearing impairment, will create a greater challenge for the educator, who may be restricted in the choice of teaching techniques.

- People with no speech can be integrated into a group, as long as the educator designs activities in which they can participate.

- In order to enhance learning, the environment needs to be a safe and pleasant one. It is unreasonable to expect participants to feel comfortable talking about sexual issues if people not in the group are walking in and out, or if there is a different worker in the group every week. The temperature in the room should be pleasant and everyone needs to be able to see any teaching aids you use. There should be plenty of room to move around when doing role-plays and other physical activities. If you are using audio-visual resources, such as a video or slides, ensure that these are set up and ready to go before the group commences so that this is not a distraction during the session.

- In order to enhance the feeling of safety and trust in the group, it is a good idea to form a group contract or agreement in one of the early sessions. The points included in the contract should be agreed upon by the members of the group and should preferably be their own ideas. Examples might be: not talking about people's private experiences outside the group, listening when other people are talking, not putting people down and so on. It should be made clear that the educator and any other staff who are present will also be bound by the agreement.

- The length of the sessions and the duration of the program need to be decided. One to one and a half hour sessions work best for most people with intellectual disability. Change teaching techniques frequently to prevent concentration from flagging and have a break or introduce a game if energy is low. Two sessions a week usually works better than one. One very short session every day is probably the best option for people with severe intellectual disability.

- Some group participants may never have learnt how to behave appropriately in a group, so the educator may need to assist group members to develop these skills.

Aims of a Sex Education Program

It is important for you, the educator, to formulate aims and objectives so that you are clear about what you want to achieve in your program. This also enables you to later measure the success of your program. This sort of measurement is called evaluation and is covered later in the chapter.

Your aims and objectives could include the information you want your group participants to learn, the skills you would like them to develop and the values you would like them to have. It is helpful to write these down as a source of reference.

Topics to be Covered

The topics covered in any sex education program should be determined by the needs of the participants. Many sexuality programs for people with intellectual disability are inappropriately focused on biological information rather than on relationship skills.

The amount of time spent on each topic should also be decided according to the needs of the participants. Remember sex education can be ongoing, throughout life. It is not necessary to cover every topic in one program. Possible topics include:

social skills
relationship skills
appropriate socio-sexual
  behaviour
sexual thoughts and feelings
sensuality
male and female body parts
puberty
sexually transmitted diseases
HIV and AIDS
sexual health
reproduction, pregnancy and
  birth
kinds of relationships, including
  those between family, friends,
  acquaintances, marriage
  partners, de facto partners and
  so on
homosexuality

sexual intercourse and different
  sexual practices
safe sex
masturbation
sexual assault, sexual
  harassment, sexual
  exploitation and incest
parenting
contraception
choices in unplanned pregnancy
responsibilities and rights in
  relationships
body image and self-esteem
legal issues
developing, maintaining and
  ending relationships
menstruation
menopause

Language

It is important that, at least initially, the educator uses the terms which are commonly used by the group participants. For example, in a session on body parts, ask participants to identify body parts using their own words. You can introduce a common terminology for the program later. Although it is important that appropriate terms are introduced, try to avoid the use of medical terminology or euphemisms.

Teaching Techniques

The teaching techniques which are most successful with people with intellectual disability are those which use a variety of audio-visual materials such as videos, films, slides, charts, posters and pictures. In the Resources section at the end of this book you will find listed a number of videos and slide presentations which have been specifically designed for people with intellectual disability. If you cannot afford to buy these (they are usually quite expensive) investigate local agencies which may lend or hire them out. Alternatively, make your own resources by sticking drawings or pictures cut out of magazines onto cardboard. If you are using them often, it may be a good idea to get them laminated.

Three-dimensional teaching resources such as lifelike dolls with genitals, or a contraceptive kit can also be extremely useful. You can find out where to get these in the Resources section at the end of the book.

The development of skills is best learnt by practice. Get your group to copy or imitate you. For example, practise putting condoms on a model penis. Use lots of role-play. Role-play is a drama technique in which participants pretend to be someone else and act out a particular situation. By exploring different roles or observing each other, group participants can learn new ways of dealing with a variety of situations. Examples could be asking someone out on a date, accepting or refusing invitations, ending a relationship or negotiating a safe sex situation. Props such as clothing can assist participants to understand that they are pretending to be someone else and can also help them to leave the role when the role-play is completed.

Take your group to visit community services such as a Family Planning or Planned Parenthood clinic. Have someone there explain how to make an appointment and what happens when they go to the clinic.

Sometimes a small panel can be an interesting and useful way to present a session. For example, you could have a panel on deciding whether or not to have children, with one person who has a child or children and one who has chosen not to have children. Another panel could be on different sorts of relationships, with a married couple, a de facto couple, a single person and a homosexual couple. Each person on the panel could talk for a few minutes followed by questions from the group. Make sure that the panel members are clear about your objectives for the session and that they are people who can relate well to people with intellectual disability.

Discussion will be difficult in groups where participants do not have discussion skills. In these groups a question and answer method of interaction may be more appropriate.

Do not be afraid to try something new. If you have a support person, talk your ideas over with him or her.

Evaluation

Evaluation involves looking back at your program aims and objectives to see if you have done what you set out to do. It is a way of measuring the success of your program.

Participants may be able to demonstrate what they have learnt by participating in a quiz or by demonstrating their skills in role-play. How you measure whether or not you have achieved your aims and objectives will depend on what those aims and objectives were.

Evaluation can be very useful for demonstrating to people who are critical or sceptical, what your program has achieved. It can also indicate to the educator which areas still need to be worked on and which teaching techniques work best.

Working with People with Severe Intellectual Disability

People with severe intellectual disability can usually learn some degree of body awareness and understanding of sexuality. Dressing and menstrual hygiene can become part of a learning process for body parts and body awareness. Some people find it difficult to see the point of a sexuality program for people with severe intellectual disability, as their possibilities for living an independent life or forming close personal relationships may be limited. But programs can assist such people to achieve their full potential and increase their self-awareness. For some people with severe intellectual disability, certain parts of sexuality programs may be better taught on a one-to-one basis.

Working with People in Institutions

If group participants have been institutionalised then it is possible that early programs may need to concentrate on unlearning certain behaviours which were acceptable in the institution but are unacceptable in the broader community because of lack of privacy.

Working with Parents and Carers

Sexuality programs are likely to be more successful when the information and skills being taught are reinforced by other people in the person's life. To this end, it is useful to have a session with parents, carers, other involved professionals and teachers, before the program begins, and again during it. In these sessions, such people can be informed about the aims of the program, the content of the sessions and the skills that participants will learn. These people will then be in a position to reinforce your teaching and improve learning possibilities.

Make it clear, however, that confidentiality forbids you to divulge anything personal said by participants during the program.

Lastly, when running programs on sexuality for people with intellectual disability, be prepared for some real highs when people make substantial progress and some times of real frustration.

Chapter 22
CHANGING INAPPROPRIATE SEXUAL BEHAVIOUR

Sexually inappropriate behaviours can be defined very differently depending on the attitudes of the carers, and on the standard of training of the residential staff. As a result, a great deal of conflict (and heartache) can and often does occur, between parents and staff, between staff themselves, and between parents of residents in the same house.

For example, the parents of one young man in a community house were able to accept his consenting homosexual relationship with another young resident, but the parents of the latter, after much anguish, decided to take him away. In a world of shrinking resources these circumstances resulted in jeopardising the community placement of one young man, and undoubtedly put further stress on ageing parents.

All too often there is a lack of agreement between caregivers and parents and other members of the community as to what constitutes appropriate sexual behaviour for people with intellectual disability.

In the past, sexual behaviour that was deemed inappropriate was often dealt with by aversive procedures. A person with intellectual disability acting in a sexually inappropriate manner was often considered to be anti-social, immoral and even deviant or criminal. In many cases, this led to any sexual expression being considered inappropriate, and an official policy of total sexual repression. Unofficially, many institutions turned a blind eye or even encouraged homosexuality, while fiercely punishing heterosexuality. Homosexuality was seen as the lesser of two evils because at least it could not result in pregnancy.

Although this kind of thinking is no longer prevalent, and although aversive procedures are no longer used to discourage sexual expression, a double standard about the rights of people with intellectual disability to sexual expression still prevails, and colours judgements about what is or is not sexually appropriate for a person with intellectual disability.

One of the problems is that sexually inappropriate behaviour can refer to anything from touching oneself on the genitals in public to rape. It can refer to a sexual behaviour which is merely embarrassing, and to the physical violation of another person. It can also refer to behaviour which exposes the person to the ridicule of others, or renders him or her vulnerable to sexual violation.

One way of getting around this problem of what constitutes sexually inappropriate behaviour, is to submit the behaviour in question to the yardstick of social acceptability. Does the behaviour make it difficult for the person to be accepted into the community? Will it make the person vulnerable to ridicule, or place him or her at legal risk? Is the behaviour hurting another, or will it make the person vulnerable to assault?

Taking the behaviour out of the realm of the sexual and into that of the social makes it easier to see it as just another set of social skills which have to be taught. Dealing with one's sexual needs is simply a matter of learning a set of development tasks, the same tasks that we all have to learn as we grow.

If a person with intellectual disability is exhibiting socially inappropriate behaviour, there are techniques which can be used to assess the reasons for the behaviour and positive behavioural and educational strategies for equipping the person with the necessary skills.

These same techniques and strategies can be used when a person is exhibiting sexually inappropriate behaviour.

The following example demonstrates some of the factors which can lead to inappropriate behaviour and shows how these can be addressed.

Peter's Story

Peter was twenty-two years old and had been living in a community-based home for eighteen months. He was charged with indecent exposure in the toilet of a popular chain restaurant.

Apparently Peter had been masturbating in the bathroom section of the toilets when a young boy came in and saw him. The manager called the police.

Peter's carers and advocate were very concerned because there was a chance that Peter could go to prison. They were also worried that Peter's behaviour might be a sign of some more serious disturbance, as Peter had always appeared to be so competent. He could converse with staff, answer the phone, do household chores and he travelled independently between work and home.

In assessing the situation, information was gathered not only about the incident, but also about Peter's level of ability, his behaviour in the home and the workplace, his interactions with other people, and his history. Several observation sessions were conducted, both in the home and the workplace, and Peter himself was interviewed a number of times so as to get to know him, give him a chance to tell his side of the story and administer some formal assessments of his intellectual functioning and his sexual knowledge.

It soon became clear that Peter's verbal ability had been considerably over-rated by staff because of his ability to mimic their behaviour and conversations. It also became clear that they had assumed far greater social experience and understanding than he could possibly have gained from fifteen years of institutionalisation prior to his placement in the group home. Moreover, Peter had not been provided with any social or living skills training before his placement, except for the travel training to and from work.

Despite this lack of training, Peter's talent for observation had enabled him to learn good survival skills but he lacked the knowledge of all the necessary sequences to be able to follow through on many tasks that should have been taught to him. Consequently, he required frequent prompting from staff and this was haphazard and inconsistent. He rarely interacted with the other residents, preferring to hover around the staff. He had very limited interests, often sitting in his room by himself, fiddling with small squares of paper that he folded endlessly.

He was known to masturbate to ejaculation in his room. He often had to be reminded to close the door when he was in the bathroom, and had the habit of going from bathroom to bedroom after a bath with no clothes on or his fly undone. As far as could be ascertained, he had not had a sexual relationship. There was some speculation that he might have been sexually abused in the past, and on a few occasions he had explained his lateness home from work by talking about a male friend or friends who had taken him to their flat, with a possible sexual connotation to the event. This was never verified.

The most important thing in his life had been his involvement with a mature married couple, with two children, who had taken an interest in Peter when he was still a child in the institution, and had had him home quite regularly on weekends. Since Peter had moved into the community, this involvement had virtually ceased.

At work Peter had to be supervised closely, because if he was left alone he would either stop work, wander about or wreck the job or some machinery while trying to do the job differently. He often said he hated work, and the foreman said he was not suited to the job, but nothing had been done about the situation.

Slowly a picture unfolded of a young man who was unhappy and bored with his work and probably his life. He had had expectations placed on him to adjust to independent living but without the training to do this successfully. Peter's placement in a group home and in a job took no account of his social needs or vocational interests, and his lack of social and sexual preparedness had been ignored. The inappropriate sexual incident seemed, on analysis, to be a logical outcome of a rather frustrating, empty and lonely existence.

Furthermore, the formal assessments revealed some specific language problems which made it difficult for him to make sense of cause and effect, and showed that he could become easily stressed by conflicting demands. He seemed particularly confused about his sexuality, and it caused him a great deal of anxiety and shame. Some of his behaviour seemed to have a strong institutional character. For instance, he was quite confused about the distinction between public and private places which would have naturally affected his judgement about the appropriateness of masturbating in a restaurant toilet as opposed to the toilet at home. He performed best when there was structure and supervision, and became confused and disoriented when faced with an unstructured setting.

It became obvious that intervention was required in every area of Peter's life. The overall recommended plan included: counselling to enhance self-esteem as well as to reinforce appropriate behaviour; training to increase personal and social skills; opportunities to demonstrate his skills and have them rewarded; broadening of his social experiences through a variety of recreational and leisure activities; and an increase in the involvement of his outside friends. Vocational options were also to be explored and he was to be given more indirect supervision. Masturbation in public toilets was addressed specifically with a formal sex education program modelling correct behaviour in public toilets, and this was reinforced by male staff and the father of his 'foster' family.

Peter's story is a good example of how sexually inappropriate behaviour can be the result of a combination of factors: a lack of understanding of appropriate social behaviour, a lack of appropriate teaching programs, and a lack of opportunities to develop his social experiences. More importantly, Peter's story illustrates the potentially serious consequences of making false assumptions about a person's level of skills, which in this case led people to ignore critical needs for education and support.

Unless a person's level of understanding and communication skills are known, as well as his or her social experiences and level of education, then it is difficult to make a realistic or fair assessment of the 'appropriateness' of a behaviour, including behaviour that is sexual.

Consider the adult man who grabs a little girl in the street, the twenty-two-year-old woman who openly masturbates in the workshop, the adolescent boy who reaches for a woman's breast in the supermarket or peers through the curtains at a female neighbour undressing. Some questions we might ask are: did they understand what they were doing? Did they have a concept of the law, or of morality, or even of social appropriateness? Were their life experiences and educational opportunities such that they could be expected to know how to behave appropriately towards others? Can it be assumed that they know, or have been taught, to deal appropriately with their sexual feelings?

The answer to all these questions might well be yes. It might even be possible that the person has mild intellectual disability and has had good social skills training and a supportive environment. If that is the case then other factors need to be taken into account, such as the mental and emotional state of the person at the time of the incident. The person's mental health may need to be considered.

If, however, the answer to any of these questions is no, and this is far more likely, then the responsibility for changing the behaviour lies with the person's parents and other carers. They need to provide the person with the necessary education and support to deal with the stresses and demands of living in the community.

Other Examples

A young woman who was visually impaired and had mild intellectual disability was driven home one night from a social function by three young men who had also been at the function. The function had been organised by a local community service for people with intellectual disability. When they parked outside her apartment block, the man sitting in the back seat with her, who had been molesting her all the way home despite her protests, proceeded to rape her. The two other young men, one of whom had Down Syndrome, sat in the front seat and sniggered.

Fortunately, she was soon able to get away and when she reached her apartment she immediately telephoned her advocate. Her advocate came over immediately and took her straight to a Sexual Assault clinic. Both the rape victim and her advocate were in great distress.

The amount of independence given to the people involved in this incident suggests that all of them were considered to be capable of a certain level of responsible behaviour. It would be interesting to know what sort of assessment was made of the level of ability, social experience, training and communication skills of the men involved, and what sort of recommendations were made by the courts regarding training and support to prevent a recurrence of this behaviour.

At the other extreme is an example of a young man in his early twenties with autism and intellectual disability, living in a group home, who developed an intense obsession about the neighbours. He would wake up in the night and shout obscenities at them through the window at the top of his voice, or climb over the fence and stand on their lawn doing the same. He then began to target certain people at his vocational centre in the same way. Usually, he was a gentle, mild-mannered man.

Naturally, the neighbours took exception to this behaviour, and they called the police.

Unfortunately, it was not possible to stop the behaviour, despite a number of behaviour programs, mainly because of the stress expressed by all parties, and the young man had to be placed elsewhere. In addition, because the level of anxiety experienced by the young man was so high, it was difficult for him to let go of the behaviour.

It is impossible to deal with every kind of problem that can arise in one chapter. The preceding examples and discussion demonstrate the variety of sexually inappropriate behaviours which can occur, and suggest that decisions about handling these behaviours can only be made after a thorough behavioural assessment.

If, after careful assessment, education and appropriate support, the particular behaviour persists, then further analysis, including medical, psychiatric and neurological may be required. Such an eventuality is beyond the scope of this book and advice should be sought from the appropriate professionals.

In general, we have found that inappropriate behaviours, sexual or otherwise, usually occur for some or all of the following reasons:

- Inadequate social skills training.
- Inconsistent support and care.
- Expectations that are too high.

- Expectations that are too low.
- Inappropriate or inadequate supervision.
- Incompatible housemates.
- Boredom.
- Not enough opportunities for social activities.
- Not enough individual choice of activities (too many group outings that are repetitive and meaningless).
- Not enough personal space.
- Frequent staff turnover.
- Poorly trained staff.
- Communication techniques not suitable to the individual.
- Serious mismanagement by carers.

In this chapter we have described ways of dealing with sexually inappropriate behaviour by people with intellectual disability who live in supervised residential settings. In the majority of cases, the inappropriate expression of sexual needs arises because education, support and opportunities for appropriate sexual expression have not been provided.

Sometimes a person with intellectual disability will exhibit sexual arousal at unusual or bizarre stimuli. This happens with non-disabled people as well. For instance, a person may like to masturbate over women's shoes or female underwear, or pictures of fast cars. As long as this behaviour does not harm anyone and is indulged in private, there is no reason to stop it. In fact, trying to prevent it may give rise to behaviours which are more difficult to manage.

This does not mean that there are no people with intellectual disability who are sexually dysfunctional or deviant in ways that are not only offensive but also dangerous — a certain proportion of any population, including the population at large, will fall into this category. But this only emphasises the importance of making a careful and detailed assessment to identify such people.

We highly recommend a very useful book by Griffith, Quinsey and Hingburger (see Resources section at the end of the book) which gives a practical model for the assessment of sexually inappropriate behaviour, and shows how to design a program to change that behaviour.

Chapter 23
SEXUALITY AND AUTISM

Very little has been written about the sexuality of people with autism and intellectual disability. One reason for this might be that it is difficult to think of a person's sexuality in isolation from a relationship, and since the most obvious impairment of people with autism is an inability to interact with people, it has sometimes been assumed that they have no drive to release their sexual urges.

However, the fact is that people with autism have a normal physical development, and display all the physical signs of puberty, with secondary sexual characteristics, including erections and menstruation. Some display an obvious urge to masturbate, and some are able to masturbate to orgasm. This means that the sexual urge is there, and although it is rarely directed towards another person, it nevertheless requires some expression or release.

At this point it may be helpful to explain some facts about autism as we have found that many disability workers know very little about this disorder.

The majority of people with autism also have intellectual disability. This means that there is almost always some proportion of people with autism in any population of people with intellectual disability, and this combination makes for specific challenges in learning and adaptation. It is very common for staff working in group homes to tell us that they are sure that some of their residents are autistic or have autistic tendencies, even though they did not come to the home with that diagnosis. This applies particularly to residents who are in their thirties or older.

Autism is a neuro-biological disorder caused by a pathology in the early development of the brain, which results in impairments in the person's ability to relate and communicate with people, and to understand and use language meaningfully. The most obvious signs of autism are ritualistic behaviours, obsessions, repetitive actions and difficulties in accepting change. These are accompanied by a distant, detached air, and an apparent lack of interest in people.

About 20 per cent of people with autism have only mild intellectual disability, or are of average or even high ability. Although such people generally have learning problems and social difficulties, they can form relationships, get married, have children and work, some in professional careers. The degree of autism can also differ, such that some people with mild autism can function quite normally.

A person with autism can also have problems in processing some kinds of sensory material, through hearing, vision or touch, and sometimes through taste or smell as well. These sensory or perceptual distortions, or dysfunctions, can cause great difficulties because they are often unpredictable and painful. Also, because the person with autism cannot usually describe his or her distress, carers and parents may be unable to find out what is causing it, even though they can see that the person is in some sort of distress or pain.

It is important to recognise and acknowledge that people with autism have great difficulty in forming relationships, and if there is intellectual disability as well, then the chances of a meaningful relationship are even more remote. Because of the nature of autism, problems in identifying with others and developing an identity are present from the start. Without a sense of self in relation to others and without the capacity to empathise, it is difficult to form close bonds with anyone.

People with autism do not understand the social cues which the rest of us depend on in our interactions, cues such as facial expression, body language, tonal qualities of voice and so on. Many of the subtleties of attitudes and emotions conveyed through such cues, are lost on people with autism.

People with autism also find it difficult to express feelings in the usual ways, and sometimes this can cause added pain and frustration. In fact, adolescents and young adults with autism often show signs of depression and occasionally are even suicidal. Those with high ability who have managed to stay in the mainstream have been able to articulate these feelings to us. They have told us how unhappy they are at not being accepted by their peer group, and at not being able to get a girlfriend because they have difficulty learning the necessary social skills.

That is not to say that people with autism do not need caring and emotional attachments. Such attachments from parents, siblings and others, contribute immeasurably to their sense of security and self-confidence. However, it is rare for people with autism and intellectual disability to be able to reciprocate in kind, or to express their need for others in a meaningful way.

Unfortunately, in practice, ignorance of social cues coupled with a profound inability to communicate can mean that feelings of anxiety, physical pain and frustration, along with positive sensual feelings, are expressed in unusual behaviours. In many cases parents and staff misunderstand these behaviours and mishandle them, sometimes with disastrous consequences.

People with autism develop physically in adolescence, and, just like other adolescents, experience the sexual needs and other physical sensations which accompany physical growth. Penile erection or vaginal secretions can lead to a need for physical relief, resulting in masturbation. Pre-menstrual tension and pain with menstruation can influence behaviour.

In general, we can begin to lay the groundwork at an early age for future education about sex. Such topics as body parts, including the sexual ones, private and public places and the different activities associated with those places, identifying boys and girls, and appropriate interaction with others, can all be introduced.

As the child develops, these concepts can be expanded to encompass masturbation in private places, and not touching people on private parts of the body.

The content and strategies of education programs will depend not only on the developmental stage of the individual child with autism, but also on the level of cognitive ability.

However, before embarking on any sex education program, it is also important to know how people with autism learn, and what their specific communication difficulties are, so that teaching methods can be adapted. Parents and teachers need to work closely in this area to ensure that teaching in different environments is consistent.

Learning for People with Autism

- People with autism are very concrete and literal; so metaphors or common sayings, such as 'pull your socks up!' will be extremely confusing.
- Their difficulties with communication mean that instructions must be brief, specific and clear.
- Instructions will work best if accompanied by materials, such as pictures, line drawings, photographs, coloured pictures cut out of magazines, or even written messages. People with autism usually relate better to visual material. One young man, for

example, could not follow a verbal instruction, such as 'make your bed', but if the words were written on a card he could do the task without any trouble.

- Some people with autism do not relate well to either verbal or visual messages, and learn best by imitating the action. You could use dolls to illustrate activities such as showering and dressing, to name body parts, or to point out the differences between girls and women. Films and videos can also be helpful.

- People with autism often have difficulty generalising a skill from one setting to another, and people differ in their ability to generalise. It may be necessary to teach the same skill all over again in a different setting. For example, the person with autism may have learnt that at home masturbation should only take place in the privacy of the bedroom, but when the need arises in the workplace, be unable to generalise the concept of privacy from the setting of the bedroom to the setting of the toilet or bathroom in the workplace.

- Many people with autism who can read do not understand what they are reading. Similarly, although they may be able to follow a spoken instruction, they may not understand why they are doing it.

- Abstract concepts such as 'love', 'responsibility', 'taking care of yourself and others', 'friendship' and 'stranger', are virtually impossible for a person with autism and intellectual disability to understand. Other words that would have no meaning are 'menstruation' and 'masturbation'. So teaching the autistic adolescent about 'stranger danger', masturbation and other such topics can be very difficult. Advice from professionals about systematic programming and alternative forms of communication can be helpful in this area.

- Routines and obsessions are often a very important component of an autistic person's life. Once autistic people have learnt a particular routine or a particular way of doing a task, it is very difficult for them to change it. Autistic people use routines and obsessions to try and impose some sort of meaning onto a confusing and frightening world. This means that it is very important to teach the autistic person the appropriate steps for any task at the outset. It can be very stressful for the person to have to unlearn those steps and learn new ones for the same task.

- It is usually not useful to teach a person with autism in a group situation. An autistic person learns best in a one-to-one situation, with many repetitions. The instructional steps must be carefully and methodically worked out beforehand, and followed consistently to minimise confusion and stress. Once learned, practice in a group may be possible.

Inappropriate Sexual Behaviour in People with Autism

Sometimes children and adults with autism behave in ways that provoke reactions of horror and distaste, because it is assumed that the behaviour reveals or will lead to some kind of deviation or perversion. For instance, if a young man masturbates in public, or pokes his finger in his anus and then smells and licks it, this may be interpreted as intentionally deviant or perverse. Extreme reactions by staff or parents, however, will only serve to reinforce or reward the behaviour and it will be repeated.

In fact, such behaviours are often only innocent expressions of sensual pleasure in the absence of any social understanding. Unfortunately, they are strongly self-reinforcing, and when coupled with strong reinforcing reactions from carers, they will become quickly established and difficult to eliminate in favour of more socially appropriate behaviours.

How best to respond to such behaviours when they begin in children? As with any problematic behaviour, it is important to avoid a dramatic reaction. In our experience, these behaviours tend to begin, not out in the community, but at home or at school, where they are easier to ignore. The next step is to redirect attention calmly to a more appropriate activity, in other words give the child something else to do.

This behaviour probably first manifests itself because something happens to direct the child's attention to the genital area. In younger children, playing with the penis, or the genital area in girls, is sometimes, although not always, associated with wetting, especially where there has been a persistent toileting problem. Playing with the anus may start when there is something causing discomfort in the anal area, such as constipation or worms. If scratching brings relief, it will be reinforced. It can then become a habit which the child resorts to, particularly when bored.

As the child reaches puberty, genital touching may be a sign of a rising sexual sensation or tension which the teenager does not understand and is exploring. In this situation, the most appropriate response is to direct the person to a private place where he or she could masturbate. If it is not possible to direct the person to a private place at that time, then redirect him or her into a more appropriate activity, preferably something fairly active which is rewarded, while ignoring the masturbatory activity.

However, a word of caution is required here. It has come to our notice that some obsessional ritualistic behaviour demonstrated by people with autism has an intense, driven quality about it, very reminiscent of the stages of sexual arousal and release. It may be that if a person in the midst of sexual tension is interrupted or redirected, his or her sexual energy becomes fixated on a replacement activity. In the non-disabled population such a transference or fixation is known as paraphilia — the person is sexually aroused by fetishes, that is objects or images which take the place of the real thing.

It is a common observation, for example, that some people with autism have quite incongruous reactions to what most people would find painful. They also receive heightened pleasure from stimuli which most people do not even consciously perceive (such as changes in patterns of light or sound), or do not notice (such as the texture of different types of cloth).

So it could be that a particular activity may provide the person with autism with intense sensual pleasure, because, during puberty that activity became associated with sexual arousal. This is particularly likely if the person does not know how to gain sexual release through normal forms of masturbation.

Since these intense obsessions and rituals can interfere with more appropriate activities, the solution may be to teach the person to masturbate appropriately so as to eliminate the obsession. The issue of teaching masturbation techniques is a stressful one for parents, and sometimes for disability workers, but where the person is clearly experiencing great agitation and frustration, it needs to be faced. This is especially so when such frustration is giving rise to inappropriate behaviour.

As with all inappropriate behaviour by people who cannot express their needs meaningfully, careful observation and analysis of the behaviour may reveal what that behaviour means to the individual, so that it is possible to appropriately and sensitively meet that person's needs.

What we do know from experience and observation is that it is far too distressing for the person with autism to try to eliminate an intense obsession altogether. It is much more constructive to gradually limit its performance to acceptable times and places, so that it does not interfere with other activities.

Sexual Behaviour in People with Autism

We have not found anything in the literature about the incidence of sexual behaviour for people with autism. In a very informal survey of one service for people with autism and intellectual disability, it was found that, out of thirty residents, five demonstrated some degree of sexual drive. In this service most of the people with autism had no or very little meaningful language or other form of communication.

One young man was known to masturbate in the privacy of his bedroom, to ejaculation, while another one frequently masturbated, but did not reach ejaculation. One young man developed an intense, obsessional attachment/fixation to a young woman at the workplace. Sometimes she allowed him to sit near her and put his arm around her, but at other times she would not. He never attempted to have sex with her, and did not appear to know what to do about the accompanying erections he was having. The unpredictability of her attention drove him to quite a frenzy, and interfered considerably in his life and work habits. The woman was eventually transferred, because she was having difficulty in coping with the advances, and his obsession faded.

In another instance, a young man had an intense obsession with another young man, and would attempt to have sex with him at every opportunity. The other man, although apparently fairly indifferent, did not object to these advances. Both men were severely autistic and also had a severe degree of intellectual disability. The men lived in the same institution, in the same ward, and it seemed likely that they had learned this behaviour in the institution.

One young woman with autism showed extreme pre-menstrual stress, but was able to learn to manage it by herself, through an excellent individually tailored program. She could request regular visits to the float-tank whenever she felt herself getting stressed, and she also went on the pill.

Despite all the difficulties that people with autism may have in dealing with the world around them, many people with autism can take great pleasure in sensual activity. For example, some people are very sensitive to touch, and to different textures. They may enjoy touching certain materials, or they may like being touched, or stroked, or rubbed. Massage, swimming and float-tanks may give them great pleasure. Others take pleasure in music, and in fact can relate better to music than to people — they find it soothing and relaxing. Some enjoy painting, pottery or sculpture, taking pleasure in the texture of the media and the sensation of colour. One autistic man has made, with help, a number of small animated films, and has sold many of his paintings commercially.

These pleasurable sensual activities should become part of the structured daily routine of every individual with autism, thereby meeting their sensual needs, and providing an opportunity for re-laxation and relief from the stress of everyday life.

However, it must be remembered that certain sensory aspects of the environment can in fact cause a person with autism considerable pain and distress. Careful observation of a person's reactions may suggest possible sources of pain, for example, lights being too bright, or flickering, as in neon lighting, some types or levels of noise, textures of particular materials in the clothes being worn, particular smells such as perfumes or deodorants, and the texture and colour of some foods. Changing some of these environmental stressors may be a simple way of relieving a person's stress, and enhancing their general well-being.

People who have a severe degree of autism and associated intel-lectual disability are becoming increasingly integrated into the com-munity. As a result, their needs for sensual outlet and for education programs which teach appropriate social and sexual skills and effective communication strategies, are becoming more apparent. Creative and sensitive programs to meet these needs is a significant and urgent task.

CONCLUSION

Sex education is about two things — facts and attitudes. The facts about sex and sexual matters are simple and straightforward. The attitudes are more complicated, because it is attitudes, and the personal and cultural values which underlie them, that cause conflicts and problems in the field.

People with intellectual disability are not a homogeneous group. They differ in their level of intellectual disability, in their understanding of abstract concepts, in the developmental level of their sexual needs and relationship skills, and in the types of experiences they have had.

These factors must be carefully assessed for each individual. They affect decisions about when to implement a sexuality program, what to teach, how to teach it, what kind of follow-up may be needed, and who should be involved in the planning and the teaching.

In this book, we have tried to say what we believe you, as parents and disability workers, need to know about sexuality, in order to ensure that people with intellectual disability are as informed as possible about the choices they need to make.

As well as this, we have tried to outline the skills necessary to achieve a rewarding and fulfilling social and sexual life.

We have also tried to make it clear that education for sexuality, like other aspects of education, is a collaborative process. It should involve a number of disciplines, because no one discipline, and no single person has all the answers, whether it be parent, teacher, disability worker or policy maker.

Parents are vital partners in this educational process, not only where children are concerned, but also where the adult has a severe intellectual disability, with or without autism, and severe communication difficulties.

Adults with mild intellectual disability should be capable of making their own choices regarding who they want to be involved in decisions affecting their lives.

Finally, the people with intellectual disability who have contributed their insights and experiences have demonstrated a central tenet of this book: that all people, regardless of their abilities, are men and women first, and that this should be the focus of our teaching. By acknowledging the sexuality of people with intellectual disability, we give them back their birthright; by allowing them to learn how to be men and women responsible for their own sexuality, we empower them to take up legitimate roles in society.

RESOURCES

Books

Anson Street Public School, *Personal Development Curriculum*, New South Wales Department of School Education, Sydney.

Designed for school-aged children.

Berwald, A. (1989) *Sexual Health: an education program for persons with an intellectual disability*, MINDA, South Australia.

This book contains a series of lesson plans in sexual health and related areas.

Berwald, A., Thornton, A. and Tustin, D. (1990) *Protective Behaviours: A Programme for Educators to Assist People with Intellectual Disability to Protect Themselves Against Sexual Abuse*, MINDA, South Australia.

Similar to scripted lesson plans.

Blum, G. and B. (1977) *Feeling Good About Yourself: A guide for working with people who have disabilities or low self-esteem*, Feeling Good Associates, California.

This book focuses on strategies for developing self-esteem and assertiveness skills in people with intellectual disability. It also covers aspects of sex education.

Craft, A. and M. (1980) *Handicapped Married Couples*, Routledge and Kegan Paul, Boston.

esearch on the nature and quality of marriages where one or both partners have intellectual disability.

Craft, A. and M. (1983) *Sex Education and Counselling for Mentally Handicapped People*, Costello, England.

Contributions from a variety of authors on a wide range of aspects of the sexuality of people with intellectual disability, including issues for parents and staff.

D'aegher, L. (1991) Sex education: teaching people with severe learning disabilities, *On The Level* Vol. 1, No. 2, pp 3–5.

Outlines teaching strategies.

Davin, L. (1990) *Going Round in Circles*, Family Planning Association of New South Wales, Sydney.

This booklet presents an alternative way of teaching Circles.

Dixon, H. (1988) *Sexuality and Mental Handicap: An educator's resource book*, LDA, London.

This book contains a series of lesson plans, mainly for people with mild intellectual disability.

Edwards, J. and Wapnick, S. (1981) *Being Me: A Social/Sexual Training Guide for Those Who Work with the Developmentally Disabled*, Ednick Communications, Oregon.

A guide for teaching appropriate behaviour.

Faith, C. (1989) *Management of Menstruation and Related Issues*, Kit No. 8, Family Education Unit, Sydney.

Contains articles on: individual family experiences, how to teach menstrual management and legal issues related to hysterectomy.

Family Planning Association of New South Wales (1991) *Double Taboo: A Course for Workers*, Family Planning Association of New South Wales, Sydney.

A sexuality teaching manual for people who train disability workers.

Family Planning Association of New South Wales (1982) *Healthright* Vol. 1, No. 4.

Edition on sexuality and intellectual and physical disability.

Family Planning Association of New South Wales (1991) On The Level: Disability and Sexuality, *Healthrites Publications* Vol. 1, No. 2.

Articles on relationships, parenting, sexual abuse, contraception and sterilisation, legal issues, HIV and AIDS, and sex education for people with intellectual disability.

Griffiths, D.M., Quinsey, V.L., Hingsburger, D. (1989) *Changing Inappropriate Sexual Behaviour: A Community-Based Approach for Persons with Developmental Disabilities*, Paul H. Brookes, Baltimore, Maryland.

For professionals designing programs for sex offenders who have intellectual disability.

Kempton, W. (1988) *Sex Education for Persons with Disabilities that Hinder Learning: A Teacher's Guide*, James Stanfield, Santa Monica.

This book is a guide for those wishing to run sex education programs and contains materials for personal values clarification, strategies for dealing with situations as they arise, teaching techniques and formal program components.

McDonald, L. (1982) A program for sex education for the intellectually handicapped person, *Healthright* Vol. 1, No. 4, pp 11–15.

How to set up a sex education group for people with intellectual disability.

McKee, L. and Blacklidge, V. (1981) *An Easy Guide for Caring Parents: Sexuality and Socialisation*, Planned Parenthood of Contra Costa, Walnut Creek, California.

Explores issues relating to sexuality for parents with a child with intellectual disability. Includes masturbation and social life.

Monat-Haller, R.K. (1992) *Understanding and Expressing Sexuality: Responsible Choices for Individuals with Developmental Disabilities*, Paul H. Brookes, Baltimore, Maryland.

A book on counselling techniques for professionals working with people with intellectual disability. It also contains some educational strategies.

Planned Parenthood of Pierce County (1983) *Personal Development and Sexuality: A curriculum guide for developmentally disabled*, Planned Parenthood of Pierce County, Tacoma, Washington.

A very comprehensive book of lesson plans covering many aspects of sex education.

Rauch, A. et al. (1991) *All About Sex* (2nd ed.), Family Planning Association of New South Wales.

A kit with loose-leaf pages containing explicit line drawings and a simple text covering all the important issues relating to sex and sexual development.

Rauch, A. (1983) Teaching Menstrual Management Techniques to Intellectually Disabled Women, *Healthright* Vol. 3, No. 1, pp 39–41.

A practical guide.

Rauch, A. (1983) Providing Contraceptive Choices for the Intellectually Handicapped Client, *Healthright* Vol. 2, No. 2, pp 41–43.

Considers the advantages and disadvantages of the various options, and the factors that need to be taken into account before a decision is made.

Rauch, A. and Young, S. (1992) *Teaching AIDS: A Manual for Disability Workers*, Family Planning Association of New South Wales.

Robinson, S. (1984) The Effects of a Sex Education Programme on Mildly Intellectually Handicapped Adults, *Australian and New Zealand Journal of Developmental Disabilities* Vol. 10, No. 1, pp 21–26.

Summary of an unpublished thesis. Research validating the fact that people with intellectual disability can learn about sexuality and that this improves their social skills and appropriate behaviour.

Whitman, B. and Accardo, P. (1990) *When a Parent is Mentally Retarded*, Paul H. Brookes, Baltimore, Maryland.

Covers educational interventions with parents with intellectual disability, issues for the children and legal and ethical issues.

Audio-visual Resources

Alexander, D. (1983) *TIPS Teaching Interpersonal Skills to the Mentally Handicapped*, James Stanfield, Santa Monica, California.

Five hundred slides and an accompanying audio-tape narration to teach interpersonal skills and social competence.

Azzopardi, S., Horsely, P. and Pietsch, D. (1990) *So You Won't Get AIDS . . .*, *STD/AIDS Prevention Education for People with Intellectual Disabilities*, Family Planning Association of Victoria.

This kit contains a video and slide set and two picture books for people with intellectual disability called *Talking About Safer Sex* and *Learning About Safer Sex*. It also contains an eight-page pamphlet called *Using Condoms*. There is some very sexually explicit material in this kit, including demonstrations of how to use condoms. A comprehensive manual for trainers is included.

Becker, O., Ellett, R. and Kerr, J. (1984) *Human Relations and Sex Education*, Kew Cottages, Melbourne.

A slide program with a teaching manual, emphasising self-awareness and relationships, for adolescents and adults with mild to moderate intellectual disability.

Brekke, B. (1988) *Sexuality Education for Persons with Severe Developmental Disabilities*, James Stanfield, Santa Monica, California.

This package consists of a teacher's guide and over 500 slides. It was specifically designed for people with severe intellectual disabilities and contains information on body parts, appropriate social behaviour, menstruation and medical examinations.

Champagne, M. and Walker-Hirsch, L. (1981) *Circles 1: Intimacy and Relationships*. This package contains a slide/sound program, photographs, teaching mat and teacher's guide. It explains the Circles Concept. Part 1 gives the learner information about social and sexual distance and appropriate behaviours. Part 2 expands the program into relationship-building skills and understanding choice and different levels of intimacy. (1986) *Circles 2: Stop Abuse* teaches self-protection skills using stories of unwanted and inappropriate touching from friends and strangers. (1988) *Circles 3: Safer Ways* teaches about STDs and HIV/AIDS. All published by and available from James Stanfield, PO Box 1983, Santa Monica, Cal. 90406.

Family Planning Association of New South Wales (1991) *The Doll's Pattern* A pattern for life-size male and female dolls with detailed genitals.

Family Planning Association of Victoria (1991) *Sexuality: Rights and Choices Drawings Set*, Family Planning Association of Victoria.

A set of thirteen line drawings of sexually pleasurable ways of touching and a range of sexual practices including masturbation and heterosexual and homosexual sex.

Family Planning Association of Victoria (1991) *Sexuality: Rights and Choices*, Family Planning Association of Victoria.

This program covers sexuality, sexual abuse and appropriate behaviour. The package contains explicit slides and line drawings covering a range of sexual activities, a teaching manual with sample programs, a picture booklet for people with intellectual disability called *I Used To Really Like Him* and an eight-page pamphlet on *Rules About Sex*.

Franing, J. *Effie Dolls*, Moline, Ill.

Small rag dolls with genitals. The female doll is pregnant.

Kempton, W. (1988) *Life Horizons I & II*, James Stanfield, Santa Monica, California.

A slide kit with over a thousand slides covering body parts, relationships, sex, marriage, parenting, contraception and sexually transmitted diseases. Includes a teaching manual.

Pictures of Health (1992) *Feeling Sexy, Feeling Safe*, Sydney.

A video and teaching manual covering body parts, and issues related to sex such as mutual consent, privacy and safe sex. There is some explicit footage showing safe sex.

Sheppard, J.L., Pollock, J.M. and Rayment, S.M. (1983) *Catch: Social Skills Kit*, Cumberland College of Health Sciences, Sydney.

A social skills program suitable for all people with intellectual disability, including those with a severe intellectual disability. Includes a training manual with scripted lessons and tapes, videos and photographs.

Social Biology Resources Centre (1990) *Janet's Got Her Period*, Carlton, Victoria.

This ten-minute Australian video is targeted at teaching menstrual management to women with intellectual disability. It uses a step-by-step approach and is very similar to the American video *All Women Have Periods*.

Western Australia AIDS Council (1992) *Safe Sex is Fun*.

This package consists of a training video, seventy-eight slides, a Makaton signing guide with new signs for sexual activities, and teaching notes.

Wish, J.R., McCombs, K.R. and Edmondson, B. (1980) *The Socio-Sexual Knowledge and Attitudes Test*, Stoelting Co, Chicago, Illinois.

Handbook for testing the level of knowledge of people with intellectual disability in many areas of sexuality.

Young Adult Institute *AIDS: Training People with Disabilities to Better Protect Themselves*, New York.

This package contains a video and manual with information on HIV transmission, instructions on condom use and advice on how to resist unwanted social pressure.

Films

All Women Have Periods 16 mm, 10 mins, USA.

A step-by-step menstrual management training film for women with intellectual disability.

Feeling Good About Yourself 16 mm, 22 mins, USA.

This film accompanies the book of the same name and demonstrates techniques for teaching people with intellectual disability self-esteem and assertiveness and for providing sex education.

On Being Sexual 16 mm, 25 mins, USA.

Parents discuss their feelings about the sexuality of their children with intellectual disability.

Agencies

In Australia your state branch of the Family Planning Association may be able to assist you with resources or trained educators. In Victoria, another agency, the Social Biology Resources Centre also has these resources. The

Family Life Movement which has offices in all states may be able to assist as well.

In the United States Family Planning is called Planned Parenthood, and there are branches in all states.

In Britain there are a number of Family Planning branches.

If a particular branch does not address the education of people with intellectual disability, they should be able to direct you to an agency which does.

There are also state and national societies for autism which should be able to help with information and resources for people with autism.

INDEX